Lost Worlds And Underground Mysteries Of The Far East

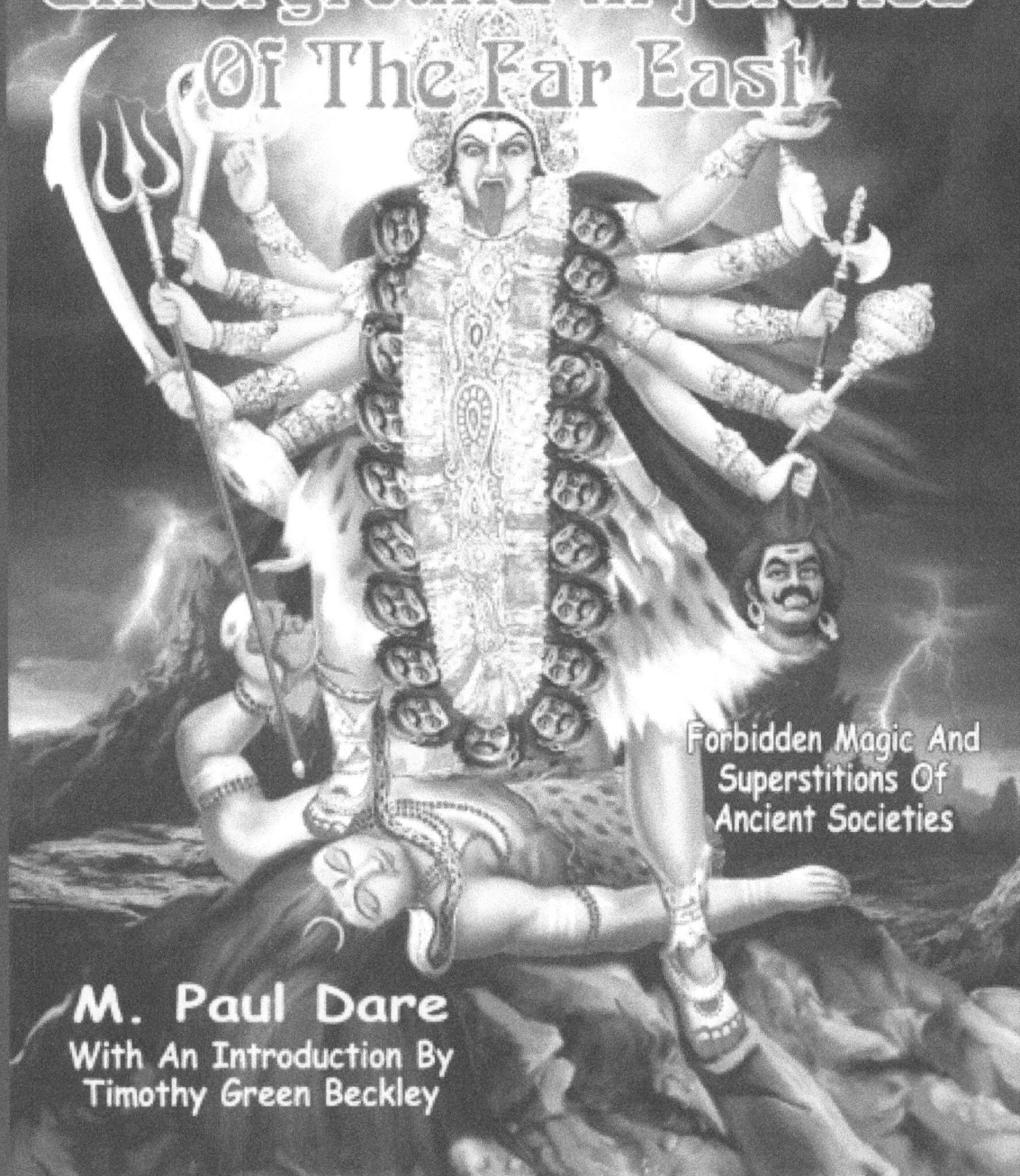

Forbidden Magic And
Superstitions Of
Ancient Societies

M. Paul Dare

With An Introduction By
Timothy Green Beckley

LOST WORLDS AND UNDERGROUND MYSTERIES OF THE FAR EAST

M. Paul Dare
Global Communications

Lost Worlds And Underground Mysteries Of The Far East

Originally published in England by the Anchor Press, 1938, under the title:
Indian Underworld: A First-Hand Account of Saints, Sorcerers and Superstitions

**New Introduction and Copyright by
Global Communications 2008**

**Timothy Green Beckley, Publisher
Carol Ann Rodriguez, Editorial Consultant
Tim Swartz, Cover Art
Typesetting, Format and Layout, William Kern**

**Timothy Green Beckley
P. O. Box 753
New Brunswick, NJ 08903**

email: MrUFO8@hotmail.com

Subscribe to our free weekly email newsletter on the web only st:
www.conspiracyjournal.com

LOST WORLDS AND UNDERGROUND MYSTERIES OF THE FAR EAST

Contents

Introduction by Timothy Green Beckley

I have been fascinated with lost civilizations and ancient mysteries since I was a kid. When I was about nine or ten, I remember seeing an ad for a company that put out intriguing sounding booklets for the price of a Coke. I waited probably two months for the arrival of several titles that you couldn't find in your bookstore (much like our titles today, except there were no web sites or Amazon.com to order from).

One of these was a 40-page pamphlet—complete with rusted staples and tiny print the title of which had originally caught my attention in the back of a Batman comic. Lost Civilizations of South America was written by Harold T. Wilkins, a researcher who spoke about dinosaurs he claimed still existed along the banks of the Amazon River in Brazil, as well as other monsters that should have been extinct a million or more years ago.

Wilkins had a way with words that had me thirsting for additional information. But there was little else that covered the subject matter that was available in my school library, or anywhere else in our tiny town for that matter. Sure there was King Kong and a few other "big ape" movies, but it was hardly the same thing.

About this time I happened to come across a copy of a magazine called MYSTIC which was edited by Ray Palmer, the original co-publisher of FATE, a digest sized magazine devoted to the unexplained which is still available today. Palmer was a slick pulp writer who knew how to turn a word.

I became fascinated and utterly intrigued by the supposedly true stories that he was spinning in regard to a civilization that existed beneath our feet in huge caverns that stretched toward the center of the earth.

Another writer, Richard S. Shaver, supported Palmer's contention that we were co-inhabitants of the same planet with an unknown race, or races, of beings. For years Shaver said that he had been fending off the negative advances of a group of subterranean dwellers known as the Dero. The Dero were a mentally degenerate group who for eons has had the utter destruction of humankind in mind.

Shaver claimed the Dero had been forced underground thousands of years ago when the lost continent of Lemuria sank beneath the sea. In addition, Palmer said that the planet Earth was hollow, had its own central sun at the planet's core and could by visited by taking a journey through vast openings that existed at both the North and South Poles.

Shortly after reading numerous episodes of this type by Palmer and Shaver, I began collecting data of my own supporting their theories and put it together into book form. The Shaver Mystery and the Inner Earth was the beginning of my career in the controversial area of what we could loosely call "conspiracy journalism."

At the tender age of 16, Gray Barker thus published my first book, which is now in its seventh printing by my own Inner Light Publications under the title *SUBTERRANEAN WORLDS INSIDE EARTH*. Some long-time readers may realize that for a couple of years I came to write regular columns for Ray Palmer's magazines *SEARCH* and *FLYING SAUCERS*. I also began a very lengthy correspondence with Shaver who had moved from Pennsylvania to Arkansas in order to get away from the Dero.

Every week he would send me a letter and a box of rocks collected from his backyard in which he claimed he could see a pictorial history of the earth's past that had literally been imprinted in the core of these stones for researchers to rediscover in this day and time.

Somewhere along the line, I also picked up a book by John Keel called JADOO that dealt with the mysteries of the Far East such as the controversial Indian rope trick and holy men who could levitate and fly through the air. Was Keel putting us on, or were all such "fantasies" possibly true?

It was all so bold and all so "far out," and it definitely changed my life. Getting into publishing on my own, I eventually began to come across other manuscripts that dealt with topics of a "fringe nature." There were books on Atlantis, on the builders of the Great Pyramids. There were dusty volumes on Tibet and on the wonders of China and Mexico. Most amazing was the fact that these works contained highly "disputed" information that ordinary texts had edited so as not to disturbed fellow academics.

What I have found is that from time to time a "lost manuscript" will resurface at a moment in history when it is better understood or welcomed than when it was originally published. The book you are now holding is one such rarity written in the early 1930's by Mr. M. Paul Dare, News Editor of the Times of India, and a very prestigious daily in its heyday.

Upon finding and thumbing through a first edition of this literary wonder far back in the basement of a used bookstore, I knew I was going to reissue it for a contemporary audience as it dealt with a part of the world that is in the headlines almost every day - but whose culture remains shrouded in mystery as it was centuries ago. Well written and well researched, this long-out-of-print book proves that sometimes myths and legends can be all too true.

Timothy Green Beckley

President, Global Communications

Preface

THE FAR EAST

Realizing how sadly large a proportion of the public has become mentally drugged and atrophied by the standardization for which the joint influence of Council-school so-called "education", the B.B.C., the cinema, mass-sport, queuing-up, and factory regimentation are jointly responsible, I have thoughtfully provided plenty of entertainment for this unfortunate majority in the opening chapters of this book.

Those of my readers who still retain intelligent interests and independent judgment, however, will find food for thought in the succeeding chapters, in which I have endeavoured to add to our knowledge of the origins of folk tales, customs, and sorcery, and in which a new view on the birthplace of Indian civilization is put forward for the first time.

That is the real object of this work. It is not, as was Katherine Mayo's Mother India, propagandist, though some of the "revelations" in my pages are equally startling to the untravelled person. The scientific student of anthropology is not interested in propaganda or sensation, and I have not thought it necessary to pander to the present taste for both by describing in lurid term even the human sacrifice I myself witnessed. Human sacrifice is just as reasonable to many peoples as eating a rabbit is to us, and we should do well to remember it.

While not concerned with politics, I take, as a student of occult ritual, the highly unorthodox but perfectly sane view that the Government of India has no business to interfere in Hindu rites which it does not understand, and of whose efflcacy it has no disproof

This will probably cause an outcry, since the political-minded must always be finding something over which they can wax controversial, especially if they know nothing about the subject; but I do not mind, so long as my readers do not deluge me with letters about it

I must express my gratitude and thanks to the very careful proof-readers of the printers.

M PAUL DARE

A YOGI BREAKING STONES BY BLOWS OF THE FIST:
MAGIC OR MUSCLE?
E.N.A.

A JAIPUR ASCETIC, REPUTED TO HAVE SPENT 30
YEARS WITHOUT LEAVING HIS BED OF NAILS. HIS
LEFT HAND IS SWOLLEN WITH ELEPHANTIASIS.
E.N.A.

E.N.A.

A HOLY-MAN DOING PENANCE ON A BED OF SPIKES NEAR KALI GHAT,
THE FAMOUS SHRINE OF KALI AT CALCUTTA.

E.N.A.

A ROLLING ASCETIC. IN THIS WAY, AN ASCETIC ROLLS HUNDREDS
OF MILES FROM ONE HOLY PLACE TO ANOTHER.

A TYPICAL FAQIR.

A YOGI MEDITATING. HE DOES NOT DESPISE THE WESTERN HURRICANE-LAMP!

E.N.A.

Chapter I

The Rope Trick and Other Mysteries

WHERE does genuine magical power end and the realm of frankly theatrical conjuring begin? This is perhaps the biggest mystery of all to be solved in probing the magical performances of "the mysterious East", and any consideration of it must inevitably involve a discussion on that perennial source of controversy, the Indian rope trick; and the author of any book on Far Eastern mysteries and beliefs feels that he owes it to his readers to start them off with this subject, since the first question always flung at anyone rash enough to admit having lived in India is: Did you see the rope trick? Can it be done?

In case there should be anyone who has so far managed to escape seeing the periodical fiery disputes on the subject in the Press, it will be as well to explain exactly what is alleged to occur in this famous performance. Briefly, the conjuror throws into the air a thin rope, or stout twine, which defies the laws of gravity by staying stiff and upright, its top vanishing out of sight in the open sky. The assistant, a boy aged about twelve, shinnies up the rope and likewise disappears. He refuses to come down despite repeated commands, so the magician, a knife between his teeth, goes up after him, and then bits of dismembered boy fall to the ground amid piercing shrieks; after which, the conjuror descends to earth, cleans his hands and the knife, and the boy appears, whole and undamaged, from among the crowd. There are variations, but that is the essence of it.

During the years the present writer worked in India the controversy became so acute, following reviews of Lt. Col. R. H. Elliott's skeptical book *The Myth of the Mystic East*, that the *Times of India* newspaper offered 10,000 rupees (about £750) for a genuine, unchallengeable performance of the trick before a public assembly in Bombay; but no Indian conjuror came forward to take up the challenge, nor has one responded to offers from the London Magicians' Circle and other bodies. There is, however, nothing surprising in this, for two reasons: one, that the true holy men of India, instances of whose undoubtedly genuine occult powers are given later in this book, do not perform for money; and the other, that the wandering Indian conjuror, even when he can read at all, which is rarely, does not read the English papers.

It will perhaps be instructive and amusing to summarize the mass of correspondence and news items which appeared on the subject in the *Times of India* and *Evening News of India* during the last burst of controversy, in 1934. The ball was set rolling by an article in the *Spectator* by Lt.-Col. Elliott, in which he discarded the evidence of a woman who declared she saw the trick in 1892 in Madras (where Elliott was then serving) because no report of it appeared in the newspapers at the time; his argument, a very thin one, was that the papers would certainly have reported such a performance. Would they? Extraordinary conjuring feats may be seen on the Maidan (an open space equivalent to a recreation ground) in Bombay any day, but the newspapers do not bother to send out a reporter, in a land where such things are as much a commonplace of daily life as murder, which has to be very juicy indeed to be worth more than a paragraph! A similar claim by a man who said he saw the rope trick in Secunderabad during the 1914-1918 war was summarily dismissed by Elliott for the same reason as that of the woman; and he was skeptical of a further account, by a woman of sixty-odd, who described the trick as she saw it when she was a child of six.

The immediate outcome of this article was that the Magicians' Circle in London, of whose "occult committee" Lt.-Col. Elliott was chairman, generously issued a challenge offering 500 guineas for a genuine performance. The famous psychiatrist, Dr. Alexander Cannon, under the misapprehension that £50,000 had been offered, was about to take up the challenge and bring over yogis who could do the trick until he discovered that the sum was only a paltry 500 guineas, whereupon he withdrew, saying it would be an insult to the yogis. All this, of course, proved nothing except the worthy doctor's utter ignorance of the habits of true yogis and their contempt for money.

Lt.-Col. Elliot characterized as "impossible" the theory which attributes a spectator's conviction that he has actually seen the trick to clever mass-hypnotism on the part of the magician; thus influenced the Magic Circle to the conclusion that the rope trick never has been done, and never will be.

Meanwhile, the controversy got into full swing in our Indian newspaper columns. Mr. G. Annaji Rao, of Bombay, declared he had seen the performance, not by a solitary conjuror, but by one of the numerous troupes of magicians in Malabar and Kanara, and he recalled the "terrible suspense" felt by himself and the rest of the audience during the performance, which, he said, took place at Cundapur, S. Kanara, in the compound of the bungalow then occupied by Mr. K. Krishna Rao, the District Munsiff (magistrate), and occupied in 1934 by a High Court advocate named S. Udpa. We will quote Mr. Asmaji Rao's own account:

"Here, then, is what actually took place, and what very often takes place down south, where this trick is of almost daily occurrence in the festive season. The drummer shouts to everyone to note that their chief is very good at bragging, but slow at performing. The urchin is then called, and told by the performer to 'go to heaven'. 'What, right up?' asks his critic.' 'And why not, when I order it?' asks the performer, cracking a huge whip. 'Why not, indeed? Then let us all go with him,' says, the critic, attempting to be jocular.

"The audience, of course, laughs, but the performer alone is stern. 'No,' he declares. 'This boy shall go alone. I order him to go. If not...' and his whip is raised.

"The critic expostulates: 'But how? Give him something to climb by, at least.' 'Well, here goes!' exclaims the performer, and with that he throws a ball of rope high in the air, holding one end in his hand. The ball mounts up, up, and up, unwinding itself and lengthening the rope as it goes, until— wonder of wonders—it is lost from view.

"I could not explain it then, being a boy. I cannot explain it now, being a man, and an old man of experience. There was no tree, no smoke (to cover the boy's disappearance), nor any cover. The ball of rope ascended the clear sky till it was lost to view. 'Now get up that rope,' says the performer, cracking his whip. The audience gapes spellbound, knowing it is possible for the boy when that man orders it.

"I feel ashamed to state what is very likely to be disbelieved. The boy caught hold of that slender rope and ran up it like a monkey. It is a wellknown trick; we all flocked to see it, and we wondered. I had developed enough skepticism even in those days, and if anyone else had told me such a thing was seen by him I should certainly have disbelieved him; but there I was, in a group of nearly 200 people of my acquaintance.

"The boy ran up the rope until he was lost to sight. Then the rope was drawn in, and the performer announced amid the thunder of the triumphant drum that he had actually sent the boy to asman (heaven). The drummer, being assured that the boy has now gone, begins to weep, and, throwing down his drum, threatens to give up service if the lad is not brought back, adding naively: 'What you can do, you can also, undo.'

"'Would that it were always so,' piously utters the chief performer; but he condescends to call back the boy, who, to the obvious relief of everyone, answers back from somewhere in the crowd, and trips up to the performer's ring."

This very clear and detailed account was followed by a brief letter from a Jubbulpore Anglo-Indian, Mr. D. Jenkins, asking Lt. Col. Elliott to "get down to brass tacks" as to whether the trick had ever been done, and find out who had seen it, before speculating on the alleged impossibility of an Indian holy man upsetting Newton's law of gravity; and the writer declared himself that he had seen the trick done three times, at distant places; further, he had the written evidence of four other persons who had seen it, with corroboration of their statements.

Another correspondent, by way of counterblast to this, drew attention to a book, **Indian Conjuring**, by Major L. H. Branson, a member of the Magicians' Circle, who devotes a whole chapter to the rope trick, stating that he had searched high and low in India for twenty-five years without ever being able to witness a performance of it, and offering a reward of 5,000 rupees to anyone who would show him the trick performed in the open; it had never, said this correspondent, been claimed. Messrs. Rao and Jenkins, however, received backing from our next correspondent, a barrister named Gulam M. Munshi, who sent in a condensed version of a letter the *Times of India* had printed' from him in 1930, when there was a previous outbreak of controversy. He declared that when, in 1895-6, he was staying at the Great Western Hotel in the Fort area of Bombay, he saw the trick from the verandah there. He wrote:

"An up-country conjuror came with a boy about ten or twelve years of age, and sat down on the path round the garden, about 15 or 20 feet from the bottom of the staircase. I was sitting on the verandah, about 30 or 40 feet from him. He performed his tricks on the open ground, with no chairs or tables, and no covering (awning) over the site on which he was performing.

"The last trick he performed was the rope trick. He threw up a ball of thin thread. The thread stood perpendicularly, without any support from the top or sides. I saw it hanging straight up. Then the boy who was with him went up with the thread. As he went up he was speaking loudly to the conjuror. His voice became less in pitch as he went up higher. In a few minutes it was inaudible. 'Then the conjuror showed his anxiety as to the whereabouts of the boy, and in a few minutes there was a noise as of something falling from above. This noise was repeated three or four times. During these incidents the conjuror declared that parts of the body of the boy had fallen from above. Then he covered these 'parts' with his basket and chanted some mantras (spells); then the boy emerged from the basket hale and hearty and salaamed the spectators in the usual manner. As it was 10 A. M. there were not many spectators."

A correspondent who used a pen-name next complained, reverting to Mr. Annaji Rao's letter, that he travelled all over Malabar regularly, and the reply he always got to repeated requests to be shown the rope trick was that only a few big conjurors could do it. "One never seems to meet these big men," he remarked. As an antidote to this there came a letter from "A European", backing up Messrs. Rao and Jenkins, and stating that he himself saw the rope trick, with the boy disappearing in the air and reappearing among the crowd, when in the Army and stationed in the United Provinces some twenty years ago.

Another correspondent spoke to seeing the rope trick done in the open in Oilmonger Street, Georgetown (formerly Blacktown), Madras, in 1892, as a boy, adding that it was so frequently seen that they did not give the conjuror any bakhshish for doing it!

After one or two letters with a metaphysical turn, dealing with the question of visual hallucination, with which I shall deal later, and a flood of jocular communications from skeptics, a Mr. V. Rebeiro came forward to say he had seen the rope trick done as a boy in the Portuguese territory of Damaun, near Bombay. He had a vivid memory of the performance, in which lie saw a fairly thin rope thrown up; the lid of an oblong basket lying near was then thrown open, and a boy aged about ten darted out of it, up the rope, and disappeared, after the conjurer's boast that he could send him to heaven and bring him back. "A minute or two later, at our earnest request," said Mr. Rebeiro, "the rope was thrown up again, and the boy down it and back into the basket. This is the real story—call it mass suggestion, optical illusion, or what you like."

A hard-headed police officer of Bangalore wrote describing the trick as he saw it at Malappuran, Malabar, on the police parade ground in 1912, in the presence of members of the constabulary. In this case there were two men, one of whom threw up a rope about thirty feet long and half an inch in diameter; a lad of about six climbed up it, disappeared in the air, and reappeared about two furlongs away. The only explanation this correspondent could get as to how the trick was done was the information, from the jugglers themselves, that they were endowed with certain supernatural powers which enabled them to make their living by this performance. Finally, a Mr. F. R. Jangalwala, of Nagpur, gave a description of the trick as he saw it at Palghat in 1921, which corresponded almost identically with the experience of Mr. Annaji Rao.

We need not take any serious notice of the arguments used by Lt. Col. Elliott, who refuses to believe the fact of the rope trick being done simply because (a) the claim to such powers is what he calls "fantastically improbable"; (b) the trick upsets the so-called laws of gravity; (c) the witnesses "failed to publish what they saw in the newspapers at the time of seeing it"; (d) the witnesses "in all cases of abnormal phenomena of this sort are generally the victims of trickery and deception"; and (e) there is no corroborative evidence.

Better arguments than these must be advanced before we can say so boldly that the whole story of the rope trick is a complete myth. As for (a), if Lt.-Col. Elliott had seen so many queer demonstrations of power in the East as the present writer has, he would not be so ready to dismiss the claim to abnormal powers as fantastically improbable; but the English military, a race heartily, and not without reason, detested by the Hindu, are the very last people to be given the facility of seeing such demonstrations. Regarding (b), not only have we no evidence that the "law of gravity" obtains utterly and without exception, but we have plenty of evidence that in certain conditions it can be upset by supernormal powers: I would here merely quote the case, classic to all students of occultism, of the medium Home's levitation, and a demonstration I have myself witnessed in India, related later in this chapter, of a *sadhu* walking across a 200-foot ravine in mid-air.

In this case I have positive evidence that there was no deception of the senses.

Argument (c) is most feeble; why, at a time when there was no Press manufactured controversy about a trick which all our witnesses above-quoted agree was commonplace when and where they saw it, should they bother to communicate an account to the papers at the time? They did so when controversy later arose. Statement (d) is a sweeping assertion on deception for which Elliott produces no specific evidence of fraud; and (e) is best answered by Mr. Jenkins's communication, stating that he had the corroborated accounts of four other witnesses besides himself.

Having so far criticized Lt.-Col. Elliott's views, it is only fair to him to say that I have never seen the rope trick myself; but have had the usual experience, which is the grievance of investigators in the matter, of only getting accounts of it at second or third hand. I have only met people who knew a third party who had seen it; this, of course, is not evidence, and there one must agree with Elliott. The nearest "contact" was a wandering Austrian artist who told me his brother had seen the trick and taken a photograph, in which neither rope nor boy appeared on the plate, though the juggler and the crowd came out clearly. This, one often hears, is the mystifying experience of other people who have tried to photograph it. In another chapter, however, the reader will find recorded a curious experience in what may be called "photo-tabu", which might cast light upon this.

The question as to whether the whole story of the rope trick is itself a myth is a very interesting one, and investigation of it takes us far back into oriental historical literature. It is often stated that the whole thing is a "yarn" invented by the famous historian and all India traveller of c. A.D. 1350, Ibn Batuta, while Chinese scholars who have gone into the matter tell me that a Chinese magician is first credited with having performed the trick, and that a distorted legend about this filtered through to India by way of the ancient Great Silk Road (rediscovered by Sir Aurel Stein), and was heard by Ibn Batuta.

It is certainly very curious that the trick does not figure in an apparently genuine list of tricks described by the Mughal historian Wahiniya Ali as being performed before the Emperor Jehangir; and what is even more curious is that the Bakhsh family, the doyens of Indian magicians, quite frankly told the American illusionist John Mulholland (who printed their statement a few years ago in the **New York Herald-Tribune**) that neither their family nor any Indian conjurors known to them had ever seen it done. As Mulholland became a kind of blood-brother of this family, he learnt many of their stage secrets.

Mr. J. D. Jenkins, however, whose letter we have already quoted, pointed out during the newspaper controversy that the rope trick is mentioned in ancient Indian literature long before the time even of Ibn Batuta, and fortunately he was able to quote chapter and verse, drawing attention to the passage, in Sutra 17 of the *Vedanta Sutras* of Shankaracharva:

"Even as the illusory juggler who climbs up the rope and disappears differs from the real juggler who stands on the ground."

He added that there is also a reference to it in the Sutras of Patanjali, and that writers in the ancient Hindu Shastras refer to the rope trick in the language of eye-witnesses.

The spring of 1935 saw a revival in London of the controversy, which, through no-one coming forward to accept the **Times of India**'s offer, had fizzled out in India. Sir Ralph Pearson, formerly Lieut. Governor of the N. W. Frontier Province, wrote to the **Morning Post** claiming actually to have seen the rope trick carried out at Dondachia, a station on the then new Tapti valley railway line in West Khandesh district, in 1900; and he added that his wife had also seen it, at another station further down the line. It is to be presumed that Lt. Col. Elliott would accept this English military man as a credible witness!

A year elapsed, then the subject was brought up again, in February 1936, in a lecture in London to the East India Association by a Major G. H. Rooke, who, while admitting that he had no firsthand evidence, stated that an Army officer was said to have taken a photograph of the performance, which plate showed neither boy nor rope. He also told a very curious story of how a friend of his, in the political service, wanted to take a photograph of a group of Indians. One of them objected, but ultimately consented to stand in the group, warning the Englishman: "You cannot photograph me!" When the plate was developed the spot where this man should have been shown was blank! This experience should be compared with that of my friend Vishnu Karandikar, related in another chapter, in his fruitless efforts to photograph a certain image.

Here, then, the matter for the moment rests, and probably will continue to rest until some genuine *yogi, sadhu*, or *faqir*, having first been obtained by the impossible method of town-crying all over India, can be persuaded to cross the "black water"—which would mean the unheard-of breaking of his caste in the case of a Hindu—to give a demonstration before the skeptical Magicians' Circle in England. Meanwhile, there does remain the question of whether we can, without prejudice, find some explanation of the mystery. The usual one, hazarded by those who very foolishly refuse to allow that an Indian holy man or magician of any kind possesses occult powers that enable him to set at defiance the phenomena regarded as "laws" in the West, is that one's conviction of having seen the trick done under one's nose is produced by clever mass-hypnotism on the part of the performer. This is too conveniently glib; it has yet to be proved that it is possible for any one man to hypnotize to the same degree, so that all see the same thing, a whole crowd of person of very diverse mental capacities.

While it is quite possible for a yogi, whose whole life is passed in the exercise of mind- and breath-control, to hypnotize a small crowd of Indian village peasants, a class whose mental calibre is extremely low, one is very dubious of his being able equally to affect such members of the audience as a hard-headed lawyer or a European police officer, and these are two types of witness whom we have quoted as seeing the trick.

I feel, however, that there may be another explanation, which does not necessarily involve supernormal power on the part of the performer. A very able German doctor practising in Bombay told me it was a proved medical fact that in the East the conscious brain, even of the European, has far less hold upon the subconscious than in Europe. In his own case this took the form of a necessity when in India to consult his text-books with distressing frequency on fine technical points of research, a thing he never had to do to refresh his memory in Europe. What, then, if this peculiar atmospheric condition makes it possible for the *yogi* or *faqir* to make you think you have seen the trick by mass-*suggestion*?

Finally, on the subject of the rope trick, since writing this outline I have met the famous illusionist Horace Goldin, who now, after many years of research, claims that he can do the trick in the open air. He showed me correspondence on his request to the Office of Works last year to be allowed to demonstrate it in Hyde Park. Naturally this was refused, since it is not permissible to have performances in any of the royal parks! Mr. Goldin has not subsequently offered to do the trick in the open anywhere else; he is a very fine showman, and a demonstration of his claim is awaited with interest by stage magicians and students of Indian magic alike.

To return, in connection with Indian conjuring, to the idea of mass-suggestion. It may sound curious to the Western mind, but there is at least one ubiquitous trick of the Indian magician in which it is pure suggestion that produces the result, following very clever sleight-of-hand. This is the famous mango trick, in which a mango plant apparently sprouts from a hand-ful of earth or sand, which, together with an old flower-pot or tin, you are at liberty to provide yourself if you think the conjuror's is doctored. It is one of the most familiar stock tricks of the strolling conjuror, and the credulous theosophist, Madame Blavatsky, was easily taken in by it (which, to those who have read her outpouring; is not surprising).

The performer, having passed a dry mango-stone round the audience, buries it in the earth or sand, waters it, and obscures the receptacle from your view by means of a light cloth thrown over a small triangle. After patter and incantations, he draws aside a bit of the cloth allowing you to see a young shoot that has sprung up, with two leaves of blackish brown. He repeats this by-play several times, until finally there stands before you, apparently grown from the mango-stone, a sapling about a foot high, with a fine cluster of genu-ine mangoes on it. The magician himself "plucks" them and hands them round for you to eat. I was once fortunate enough to be able, from a concealed vantage-point, to focus a powerful pair of field-glasses on the finished prod-uct while the conjuror was concluding his patter, in which he made the usual boast that if you cared to wait long enough he could grow a mango-tree twenty feet high; and the glasses revealed plainly that, the mangoes had been most ingeniously tied on to the stem by a lightning sleight-of-hand many a Western stage conjuror might envy. The leaves and stem are tough, and their concealment, even in a loincloth, presents no problem to the In-dian performer. Now, the curious thing about this performance is that even Europeans who had been watching it closely declared afterwards that the stem did grow up out of nothing under the cloth, while five Indian spectators to whom I spoke after the conjuror had packed up and departed, well re-warded, were convinced that he had grown a mango tree twenty feet high. It was all pure suggestion.

I had an even more extraordinary personal experience of the power of suggestion from a Purijabi *faqir* with whom I was very friendly, and who taught me a number of his "stage secrets". This man, while declining to commit himself on the subject of the rope trick—he would not even say whether it could be done or not, let alone how it was done—admitted that many of his own tricks, and those of all his fellow conjurors, are worked purely by suggestion, without even troubling to use hypnotism properly so called. One day he gave me a demonstration, seated in a corner of my bungalow lounge, and with my own property. In the opposite corner from where we sat side by side on the mats stood, on its wooden stand, a large brass tray of Jaipur-ware, with a very heavy brass vase to match in its centre.

"Now, sahib," said my *faqir*, "I can will that vase to ascend from the tray to the ceiling."

The vase thereupon rose gracefully into the air before my eyes, and I actually heard the metallic tinkle of its lid touching the ceiling.

I now will it to descend," said the magician, "and to halt a short time in mid-air on the way down." It did, and again I heard the tinkle when it touched the tray on coming down.

"Now, sahib, " said my old friend, with a mischievous grin, "I will do it again. This time, while the vase is in mid-air, please walk across the room to the tray."

I did, keeping my eyes glued on the vase, which, defying Newton and all his works, remained parked in mid-air without visible means of support, and steadily nearing the ceiling again.

"Please put out your hand to the middle of the empty tray, sahib."

I obeyed-and touched the vase, which at the same time seemed to vanish from above my head. Bewildered, I turned round, exclaiming that I could have sworn the thing had been mid-air over my head a second before.

"That sahib, " smiled the old fox, "was the suggestion. The vase has never left the tray."

It only remains to add that this wily old conjuror, a familiar figure on the sands of Juhu, Bombay's lido, disappears from his native shores every monsoon to perform on the halls in Europe, where he has picked up perfect French and Italian, good German and passable fortune by his art.

My wife had an experience similar to mine, though perhaps it comes nearer the realm of actual hypnotism, while staying for a short time at

Ganeshkhind, where one afternoon an old *sadhu* entertained a small circle of friends in the garden of Government House. Among other things he made them believe that bananas were growing in luscious clusters on a tree known to have been long barren. One of the officials present even sent for the *mali* (gardener), who, on seeing the bananas, expressed his astonishment that the tree had borne fruit overnight. He was told by the *sadhu* to get a ladder and cut a bunch. The man went up and sliced carefully at what he judged the finest bunch of the lot, then let out a yell of terror and nearly fell off the ladder, shouting: "They aren't there!" All the Europeans watching, except my wife, whom it is impossible to hypnotize, swore they saw a bunch of bananas fall to the ground when the *mali* sliced at them; needless to say, on inspecting both the tree and the ground beneath it, there was no sign of a banana on either.

The holy man next gave the party a scare by willing a cobra to appear at their feet from under a few leaves on the gravel path in a part of the grounds where snakes were never seen — apart from the fact that a snake will not go over gravel and similar rough surfaces. Having found it impossible to subject Mrs. Dare to hallucination, the *sadhu* asked if she would object to the snake going over her feet, to prove it was real. She consented, remarking that she knew she would not be able to feel the creature; and on looking down she actually saw it sliding across her feet, but did not feel its cold skin, though wearing open sandals and no stockings. As the king cobra is the only known snake of India which will attack a human being on sight without provocation, the rest of the party had an unpleasant few minutes of apprehension; but the brute was then permitted by the *sadhu* to depart into the shrubbery, whither it went with a very realistic rustling, and to this day we cannot decide whether it was a real snake or an image-projection.

When all the cases of suggestion, hypnotism, and sleight-of-hand have been ruled out, however, all who know the East, and who do not possess a biased, bull-headed mentality, are bound to admit that there is left in all oriental magic a very considerable residuum only explicable by allowing to its exponents the possession of supernormal power, that can and does set at defiance those "laws" which the West, in its self-sufficiency, thinks are immutable.

Although falling outside India, it cannot be out of place here to cite that classic case, known to students of occultism and actually on record in the sober annals of the *Sürete* (the Scotland Yard of Paris), the case of the transported portrait. This occurred only a few years ago in the French Congo, where a district administrator, hearing tales of the great powers possessed by the local witch-doctor, was skeptical, and went along to his hut to tell him so and challenge him to a demonstration. First the witch-doctor bade him think of someone he knew very well; the official thought of his fiancee, where-upon the medicineman, who could not read or write, spelt out the name of the woman in roman capitals with his stick in the sand. "This," he said, "was too easy — just mind-reading. Think of some object in your house in faroff Paris that you much prize."

The administrator concentrated his thoughts on a valuable old master, a portrait hanging in his Paris home, without, of course, telling the magician of what he was thinking.

"Look," said the old man, "there is your picture." And there, standing in a corner of the mud hut, was the picture.

The French officer declared it must be hallucination, but the witch-man shook his head. "No," he said, "it is real — go and pick it up for your-self." The amazed European walked across the hut and actually picked up the picture, complete in its familiar frame, which he thought was hanging in his home thousands of miles away.

He thought he must have caught a touch of the sun. Dazed, he dashed down to the station telegraph-office and fired off a wire to Paris inquiring if this painting were still in its place. Fairly quickly there came a reply stating that it had been missed shortly before his cable arrived, and that the Süreté was at that moment turning the place upside-down investigating the theft, as the portrait was of great value.

Still more dazed, the official collected a number of reliable European acquaintances and friends, who accompanied him back to the witch-doctor's hut and there saw for themselves the picture still standing in the corner. Some of the men were brother-officers, who had actually seen the thing in the house in Paris when on leave. They wanted to pick it up, but the medi-cine-man would allow only the owner to do that.

Finally, the magician was asked how long he could keep the picture there, and replied, "Till sundown." Returning just before sundown, the Frenchman confirmed that his treasure was still there; and as the sun sank it melted into thin air before his eyes. He at once cabled Paris again, asking if the picture had yet been found, and in due course came the reply that it had mysteriously reappeared in its accustomed place, while the Sureté was still combing the underworld of the Parisian antique-dealers for it. The family thought a servant had tried to purloin it, but had lost courage at the police activity and replaced it on the wall.

Almost as queer was a feat witnessed on the Indian frontier by one of my colleagues, who, when serving there in the Army, himself assisted in the performance. One evening, he relates, a genuine *faqir* strolled into the camp and, declining reward, offered to entertain, saying money meant nothing to him, and he would merely ask a little food if they were pleased with what he could do. The officers sat in a semicircle, the *faqir* some thirty feet away from them; he said he would not move, or even touch anything involved in certain tricks.

After a number of minor stock feats he asked for the use of a very distinctive ring the colonel was wearing, which bore his monogram on a shield-so that no substitution was possible, as might have been the case with a plain gold band. The faqir asked the colonel to hand the ring to any officer he wished. He chose the adjutant, who was then requested by the conjuror to find any bit of paper and screw the ring up in it, under the eyes of yet two other officers (of whom my narrator was one). This done, the adjutant was told to throw it down a thirty-foot well, at least twenty feet from where the *faqir* was sitting, the two other officers acting as witnesses. My colleague vouches for having tested that the ring was really screwed up in the bit of newspaper, and for seeing and hearing it flop into the water of the well, where it sank.

The *faqir* next asked the colonel to send for a mess orderly and tell him to bring a new, uncut loaf: This was done. "Now," commanded the magician, "cut the loaf; and you will find your ring inside it." And the colonel did! There is no explaining a feat like this by any theory of hallucination or hypnotism; the *faqir* touched nothing whatever in the performance, and it can only be explained by a frank admission that some of these holy men of India do actually possess the power to dematerialize and rematerialize objects at a distance. There was living at the Railway Colony, Sukkur, Sind, in 1934, an occultist calling himself Muzzaffer (which means "the traveller"), who in that year proved his powers to a skeptical Hindu merchant of my acquaintance by emptying that worthy's office safe, which was in an office over a mile away from where they both were at the time, and rematerializing the whole of its contents, including heavy ledgers, under the astonished trader's nose. He was even able to confirm the genuineness of the feat by telephoning his clerk on the spot to open the safe; the latter did so, and 'phoned back in great distress that it had been burgled, though the lock was intact. His employer reassured him, explaining the position. Muzzaffer then "dematerialized" the property again, and on the merchant then telephoning the clerk to reopen the safe, that astonished individual reported that the whole of the contents were back in it, apparently undisturbed.

Then there is a celebrated, and perfectly true, story of a *sadhu* in a Madras gaol, sentenced to a short term for theft, who completely mystified warders and officials by being found each morning seated in an attitude of meditation outside his locked cell, with the lock untouched. This Indian Houdini threatened that this would happen every day unless they ceased to "insult" him by locking the door; so it was left unlocked, and the man completed the rest of his sentence in sublime peace, never attempting to escape. It is such occurrences as this which cause one to wonder how much of the great Houdini's own escapology was pure science and lockbreaking, and how much he may have learnt, from his Eastern mentors, of other and more occult methods. His own book does not reveal the answer, but Indian magicians with whom I have talked tell me he was the only Western adept who ever mastered these secrets.

Mention of Houdini brings us to another of the great puzzles of Indian magic—the claim of *yogis* to remain in a state of suspended animation for an almost incredible period. Houdini himself undoubtedly learnt part of their secret, but not all of it, for he has left it on record that his narrowest escape from death was on the last occasion he ever consented to be buried alive in a coffin, in a six foot grave. He confessed that his nerve failed him, with the result that he nearly did expire.

An oriental scholar and artist with whom I became very friendly in India, Mr. Fyzee Rahamin (the Bombay painter responsible for some of the New Delhi frescoes), told me of an amazing case, to which he himself was witness, that occurred some years ago in the State of Rampur, where the records of it exist, duly attested by the official doctors and a number of scientists. Here a *yogi* insisted on being buried for a year and a day. He went into *samadh* (trance), and was certified to be dead, medically speaking, and by all known tests; and he was interred in a proper grave six feet deep. Mr. Rahamin was present at the interment, and at the exhumation of this living saint a year and a day later, and states that when the coffin was opened the man got up, emaciated, but otherwise well and normal, after taking some two hours to come out of his *samadh*. This is no ordinary case of catalepsy, the longest recorded duration of which is a few days.

In the same class of supernormal phenomena may be placed levitation, of which the first demonstration in the West under test conditions satisfactory to science was the now classic case of Home, the American medium, who rose from his chair in a fifth-floor flat, straightened out into a horizontal attitude above the heads of the observers, departed feet foremost out of a window, and re-entered the room head first, still horizontal, by the next window. This is a well-attested case in western psychic annals, and at the time it naturally caused a sensation, but to the *yogi* it is almost a commonplace, everyday accomplishment.

I was personally given a demonstration of it by a learned Swami, or teacher, of the colony of holy men who live in the caves of Jogeshwari, near Bombay. He stood discussing these phenomena with me on the edge of a 200-foot ravine, smiled very sweetly at the western skepticism expressed, and then proceeded to walk across the ravine in mid-air. This was certainly not hallucination. He had definitely left my side, and was talking to me the whole time he was "levitating". Arrived on the far brink, he turned round, delivered himself of a few home-truths on the subject of western science, and returned. This man is a very great scholar, with a complete contempt for the bestial accretions with which the teaching of Hinduism has become overlaid, and, incredible as it may seem to a prosaic Londoner, not only claims to be over 150 years old, but can prove it by records, and looks no more than sixty. I leave it to the reader to "believe it or not", only cautioning him against the inconsistency of admitting the claim of Christ to walk on the waters, and yet denying the possession of similar power to other oriental adepts in the occult.

Our old Arab traveller, Ibn Batuta, cites the case of a *yogi* who took the form of a cube at will, while a story savouring strongly of the Arabian Nights is told by another Muslim historian, Mas'udi, concerning a certain Jew of Surarah, a village in Kufa district. This man raised a number of apparitions, and made a phantom king of colossal size gallop on horseback round the mosque courtyard at Kufa. In the presence of Walad-ud-Din Akbar he then turned himself into a camel and walked on a rope; made the "ghost" of an ass to pass through his body; and finally slew a man, cut off his head, passed the sword over head and body, and reunited them, so that the man lived again. This last feat very much recalls our Indian rope trick, and it is even more strikingly reminiscent of certain feats performed many centuries before in ancient Egypt, according to a papyrus describing a magical performance said to have been given before the pyramid-builder Khufu.

With regard to the claim of the yogis to perform levitation and suspended animation, Major Rooke, to whose lecture we have alluded, gave much evidence which, while he claimed no first-hand knowledge, led him to conclude that these feats are actually accomplished, and that the secret lies in constant practice of the subjection of mind to matter, and the cult of will-power. This, indeed, is the chief object of Yoga, the Hindu "science of breath", and most of Hindu occultism may, without any disparagement, be described as methodical self-hypnosis to induce a state of ecstatic contemplation. All the training of the potential *yogi* is directed towards this, the concentration of the will, and the subjection of the conscious personality and material self to the subconscious, leading ultimately to Sat-Anandi, the Supreme Bliss, a spiritual state similar to that called by the Arabs Kkayf, for which there is no adequate word in English.

Mokam Singh and Pandit Panna Singh, two yogis who made a world tour in 1934-5, state that in Tibet they met yogis 200 years old.

Les Prairies d'Or (Ed B. de Meynard & P. de Corrtaille) Paris, 1863. Tome ii, 398 seq. (Kitab murujadh-dhahab).

The basis of the several Yoga systems appears to be the intention to liberate what western psychists call ectoplasm (which has been actually photographed by German scientists as a kind of aura surrounding the body and taking its shape at the point of release) by a system of concentration on certain nerve-centres, aided by rhythmic breathing and the repetition of certain phrases and incantations to the point of self-hypnosis. The Buddhist monk's constant repetition of the sacred *Om mani padmi Om* is an illustration; it is based on knowledge of sound vibrations, that of *Om* being held the symbol of world perfection. It is rather curious that the six nerve-centres on which concentration is made are as familiar to the Guatemala and Yucatan Indian witch-men, and to the Zoroastrian mystics, as they are to the student of the Hindu occult teaching.

I can assure anyone who cares to try sitting for half an hour in one of the attitudes so familiar to us in the statues of Gotama Buddha that, to begin with, it is extremely painful, producing the sensation known as "pins and needles", felt when one's foot "goes to sleep". The Yoga system deliberately induces this condition, and as each of the six nerve-centres controlling different limbs and functions is put to sleep, the ultimate result is a rigid state corresponding to what one may term localized catalepsy. That is why Indian fanatics are able to hold their arms rigid for days without tiring, and why they can produce prolonged states of trance.

Here we come to the darker side of the subject, the very real and terrible black magic of India; for in this strange land, where the highest spiritual truths not only walk side by side with darkness and bestiality, but in many cases are even wrapped up in, and symbolized by, grossness, the two are linked in the practice, by evil adepts, of the lowest form of Yoga, the *Prayanayoga*, whose powers are obtained by intense concentration on the lowest of the six nerve centres, that of the sexual organs. There are some aspects of this black magic, and its technical details, which the present writer, in common with others who have made a long study of oriental occultism, declines to publish, feeling that such knowledge is best lost to the world; but there are other features of it whose recital is not only harmless but instructive to the student of anthropology and belief and to these we will now turn.

Chapter 2

The Superstition Racket

A PART from the many strange occurrences to be found in India which, as we have seen, do admit of serious inquiry by students of occultism, there is a side to the widespread belief in the supernatural which becomes frankly amusing, but which cannot be altogether ignored even by the student, for the credulity it reveals naturally has to be taken into account in assessing the credentials of more serious happenings.

Modern America is usually supposed by Europeans to be the birthplace of what is vulgarly known as the "racket", but it must surely give the palm to venerable India, where they have a racket more novel in character than any yet tried in America, with the possible exception of the foundation of crank religious sects for which the United States are famous.

This is the superstition racket, most lucratively practised by astute rogues and vagabonds in the guise of the holy man, styling themselves *sadhu* or *faqir* according as they be Hindu or Muslim. The chronic extent to which the Indian mind is gullible may be judged from the fact that the Penal Code actually contains a section providing for the punishment by the courts of anyone who "induces a person to believe that he may become the object of divine displeasure"; and very illuminating are some of the cases of the superstition camp that actually came before the courts during the time I was working in India.

One of the most ingenious of such cases occurred at Nagpur in October 1934, and the sessions judge made strong comments on the credulity of the Indian rustic.* He had before him the appeal of four men who had been sentenced for fraud—which sounds prosaic enough until we see how the fraud was accomplished. It appears that the news spread round the Central

Provinces village of Wandongri that a deity named Mahishur Dev was going to make a "personal appearance" in the district to cure the defective eyesight of a woman, the wife of a peasant named Pandaria. In case a large crowd should gather and perhaps become a little unruly by reason of religious fervour or toddy-drinking, or both, the local police subinspector decided to be present at the demonstration of the miracle.

The alleged god, clad impressively in black, duly made his appearance at the appointed time, and the villagers started doing *puja* (worship) to secure his blessing. In the crowd were two men named Gangaram and Shripat, who subsequently found themselves in the dock on a charge of complicity. Mahishur Dev, in sepulchral tones, duly offered to cure the woman's eye disease completely, but no one except the observant police officer seemed to think it at all curious that a god should, as he did, demand a fee of ten rupees as time for his cures. The amount was paid up, whereupon the supposed deity did a most ungodly and athletic sprint. Then the villagers realized that all was not as a should be, and chased him. On being captured the "god" was unmasked as a man named Sudama; the ten-rupee note and his black get-up figured as exhibits in court!

Investigation revealed that his modus operandi was to go round the villages in this attire, his accomplices having first salted the ground well by wondrous tales of the god's healing powers, and his promise to appear. A magic line was then drawn, beyond which the villagers must not go, on pain of being devoured by a demon, while the "cures" were in progress. This, of course, was to facilitate the quick getaway. A man named Sadashive aided in the game by commanding the god to appear at a magic summons.

In the appeal court this man's sentence of a year's gaol was upheld, but that of Sudama was reduced from two years to one, and Gangaram, and Shripat were acquitted for want of evidence. The judge observed: "The faith of simple villagers is so boundless that what might appear to a civilized man foolish may appear full of sense to them. There is not the least doubt that the people of Wandongri honestly believed the apparition was really Mahishur, and made offerings in that belief"

* *Times of India, 1 Nov., 1934.*

Even a large modern city like Bombay is by no means free of such extraordinary credulity, as witness a case in March 1934, when a man who claimed that he was a *bhagat* (magician), and could at will take the life of any person by black magic, was sentenced to a day's gaol and a fine of 200 rupees, or four months' imprisonment in default, at Dadar police court on the prosaic charge of cheating.* This man, in collusion with two others, deprived an ignorant cottonmill worker of 750 rupees by posing as a magician. His accomplices approached the victim, telling him they were the employees of a rich merchant living at Walkeshwar (the West End of Bombay), who wanted to get rid of his adopted son at all costs. They asked the victim if he knew of any magician who could help in the matter, and promised a large reward.

The next step was that the alleged *bhagat* made the acquaintance of the victim and impressed him as a sorcerer, being consequently recommended by him for "job" at Walkeshwar. Some days later the accomplices sought out Krishnaji, telling him that the merchant's adopted son was dead as the result of the magician's art, and they brought a bundle which they said contained 20,000 rupees, the promised reward to the mill-hand. Before giving him the parcel, however, the swindlers asked him to give them 45 rupees for stamp money, and a cheque for 700 rupees; this he managed to raise from his friends. The racketeers took it and vanished, and, of course, when the simple mill-hand opened his parcel it contained only slips of crisp blank paper.

The success in India of one of the most common forms of swindling, by trading on a belief in magic, is due almost wholly to the Indian's chronic love of money. It used to be said that you could get a murder done anywhere in the country for 40 rupees; I believe it is now much cheaper! The word paisa (cash) is the most frequently heard in any conversation, and the subject is the cause of most of the quarrels that break out every five minutes. Even shrewd moneylenders and stockbrokers, accustomed to piling up wealth themselves by every known questionable trick, seem to "fall" for the many variations of India's prize confidence-trick: how to get your money doubled. One Bombay merchant I knew was so shrewd that he had made a fortune of over ;£2,000,000, yet so mean that, clad in a disreputably dirty *dhoti* and shabby sandals, he would haggle with a gharry-driver over two annas in the amount of a fare, and was once handsomely rooked of jewels worth some £3,000 by the ancient trick of gold-multiplying!

Times of India, 24 March, 1934

There was a great ramp in this form of criminal activity in the town of

Surat in August 1934, which only came to light when one of the victims, a Hindu woman, went to the police, the others having kept quiet for fear of being made to look foolish through the publicity of a court case.* An extraordinary story of an elaborately stage-managed performance in alchemy was revealed in court. The woman was supplying passers-by with water when a *sadhu* (as she thought) approached and spoke appreciatively of her benevolent work. In recognition of her services to mankind, he said, he proposed to give her a quantity of gold to utilize for religious purposes, and he further revealed that he would do this by causing whatever gold she herself possessed to be doubled.

Next day he turned up and asked her to supply him with pieces of gold, silver, and copper, which she did. He then prepared a small furnace of mud and put the metals into it, together with some powder and pills, as the result of which a large piece of gold, certified by a jeweller as genuine, came out of the furnace when it was cooled down.

This, of course, inspired confidence. The *sadhu* departed, saying he would return next day and make more gold. The woman, believing he had supernatural powers, offered him, on his return, all her gold ornaments, worth about 500 rupees, tempted by the prospect of getting back their value 100 per cent. The so-called holy man performed much hocus-pocus, chanted incantations, prepared a big furnace, and apparently put all the ornaments into it in a big pot, with bits of copper. He then asked the woman to fetch some flour and molasses. This she did, and from them he prepared an image of the elephant-god Ganpati, or Ganesh, which he placed near the furnace as a symbol of good luck and wealth. After this he departed, promising to come next day and open the furnace. Of course he did not, and the poor woman, growing suspicious, opened the furnace herself only to find the pot empty and her jewels gone. She did not at once inform the police, but kept her eyes open, and six weeks later caught sight of the *sadhu*. Confronting him, she demanded her jewelry, whereupon he turned and bolted, but was seized by passers-by.

Times of India, 28 Aug., 1934.

A similar incident occurred in a neighbouring town, Rander, where another *sadhu* robbed a gardener of the whole of his life savings, about 600 rupees. These were simple country folk, but the hard-headed Marwari class, whose god is money, prove equally gullible. A case occurred in April 1934 at Hyderabad, Deccan, capital of the Nizam's dominions, where a wealthy Marwari merchant, living in the Sultan Bazaar, complained to the police that he had been robbed of jewels worth 8000 rupees by an astrologer's confidence-trick. The reader of stars (who, by the way, was not caught) called at the Marwani's shop, waved a coconut round the victim's head, mumbled spells over it, and broke it open, whereupon a liquid the Marwari thought was blood spurted forth from it. This bit of stage conjuring convinced the Marwari that the man possessed magical powers.

Seeing that he had created a deep impression, the astrologer offered to double all the jewelry in the Marwari's safe. The merchant allowed him to inspect the jewels, all of which, he swore, were then securely locked up again in the safe. The astrologer, after muttering divers incantations, said he would return again next day, and that if the Marwari then opened the safe again he would find double the amount of jewelry in it. The man did not return; doubts assailed the merchant and he opened the safe, to find it empty.

To anyone who has seen the marvellous sleight-of-hand performed by Indian conjurors, as, for instance, in their mango-tree trick described in our first chapter, it is not at all surprising that the astrologer managed to make off with the trinkets from under their owner's nose. Nor is it very surprising that a business man should have been gulled despite the frequency with which such cases are reported in the papers, for Hyderabad is a god-forsaken place to reach, and few of these merchants, for all their wealth, are literate; and, moreover, the least "odour of sanctity" completely asphyxiates their sharper senses!

These "doubling" tricks occasionally lead not to a prosecution, but to a civil court suit, in this land of queer anomalies. Thus in June 1934 a plaintiff sued for recovery of an amount which, he alleged, he had handed to the defendant to be taken to a magician for the purpose of being multiplied tenfold, at Sinnar.* The aggrieved one alleged that the defendant, a relative who lived in the same village, told him that there lived at Jayagaon a magician who turned every 100 rupees handed to him into 1000 rupees by the exercise of his black arts.

The plaintiff seeing a chance to get rich quickly, sold his patch of land for 200 rupees and handed 150 rupees to his relative for the purpose of getting the magician to multiply it to 1500 rupees. He told the court that he neither got back his original capital nor received the magical increase, so he promptly sued his relation for the original 150 rupees. The defence made a complete denial of any such transaction, or even of being handed the cash. The defendant added that a magician from Jayagaon went to the village and deceived a number of people by a similar confidence-trick, but that he (defendant) had nothing to do with it; and finally he advanced the subtle argument, worthy of a Jesuit seminary, that even if the plaintiff had advanced the amount to him it was irrecoverable, as it was advanced for a purpose the law held illegal!

There seems no end to the variety and ingenuity displayed by the rogues and vagabonds of India, in the guise of holy men, to part fools rapidly from their money. The lure of buried treasure is a frequent bait, easily swallowed owing to the habit in many parts of the country of burying one's valuables under the earthen floor of the hovel to safeguard it from wandering bands of dacoits, the highway robbers who frequently cut the throats of everyone in the house, then dig up the whole floor searching for gold and jewels. Hence, if a man is told treasure is buried under the house he is occupying, it does not sound very fantastic.

Times of India, 27 June, 1934.

From Kasur, a Punjab town in Lahore district, there came an amusing story in April 1935 of how a Harijan (a member of the outcaste depressed classes, regarded as pariahs by the caste Hindu) swindled a Muslim, who got the idea there was treasure buried beneath his floors, but did not know exactly where to look for it.* Hearing of this foible, the wily Harijan approached the Muslim, who, of course, had no caste scruples about contact with a man of this class, and told him he had received an astrological revelation that treasure was undoubtedly buried there. Not being very well up in astrology, however, he said, he would offer to bring his guru (religious teacher) to the house, as the latter would by divination be able to indicate the exact spot; and doubtless the follower of Allah would mark the service by a little present?

The Muhammedan agreed, and the swindler thereupon brought along another Harijan, whom he introduced as the holy guru, safe in the knowledge that one who was not a caste Hindu would not detect the fraud. The second conspirator performed divining hocus-pocus, and finally ordered that a certain spot in the floor be dug, declaring that treasure would be found below. He told the Muslim to fetch a white hen and fifteen tolas of gold (2700 grains). Building castles in the air, the old fellow dashed off, procured the hen, and also laid hands on all his wife's jewelry. The pseudo-guru sacrificed the white hen in the hole, muttering impressive spells the while; after which he asked the Muslim to watch the hole, saying he would complete the process of divination in a near-by stream, into which he would throw the sacrificed hen. The other Hindu also departed, on a pretext of getting something requisite for the ritual. Needless to say, they did not return, and after dutifully watching the hole in his floor for some time the Muslim became anxious and inspected the box in which he had brought his wife's jewels, to find it empty.

Evening News of India, 9 April, 1935

Apart from its illustration of human gullibility, this affair has a moral, which is that no true Muslim ought to countenance rites involving the universal Hindu sacrifice of poultry; but Islam in India is extraordinarily full of Hindu superstitions and corruptions.

Occasionally we do meet with a case of treasure-hunting into which supernatural powers appear genuinely to enter, when there is no question of divining, either real or pretended, being used. Such a case occurred in Thaton, Burma, in January 1934, when a search was made by digging in front of the Indian cemetery for the treasure of a Karen family who escaped, after burying it, in the Shan rising of half a century ago in Tenasserim.*

* Times of India, 6 Jan., 1934*

One of the surviving sons of this family, eighty years of age, told a friend named Saya U Thaung Pe that they buried their valuables under a sawmill in Thaton and evacuated the village to go to Kyauktalone, five miles away; so Saya offered prayers to the spirits to be shown the actual place where it was buried, and they are said to have shown him the spot, with the result that he and the family gathered a party, dug there, and found the valuables concealed under big flat stones.

Equally inexplicable was a curious incident which occurred in November 1934 at a village called Duramari, fifty miles from Gauhati, where the foundations of a stone-built temple containing three images of the god Siva were discovered as the result of a dream. Bhagavati, a form of the mother-goddess, appeared in a dream to a villager, and indicated a spot at one corner of the local *ghat*, or sacred tank, as the site of a temple; and when the man and his neighbours excavated there, they actually found the remains.

So far as I can discover, there was no record of the temple's existence, and the only local tradition was that the tank had been made ages ago by a Hindu king called Arimatta, of whom the villagers knew nothing.*

Times of India, 15 Nov., 1934

We must now return to our swindlers. It is not always that visions come off so happily, and they sometimes end in civil lawsuits which provide a welcome comic relief to the way in which religion and crime intermingle in the more sordid setting of the police court. The most famous of such suits in modern times was a case which dragged on for years, and was still in progress when I left India in 1935; in it a motor-driver of Amritsar, in the Punjab, sued his *guru* for alleged failure to carry out a promise that he, the driver, should see God face to face-which unique experience, apparently, had been promised the driver in many weird and wonderful visions. Not only did God most disobligingly remain invisible after eight years of laborious search, but the driver, in the first completed stage of the affair, was ordered to pay damages to the sage, who was the head of the Radhaswami sect of Hindus.*

Ibid., 13 June, 1934.

Bold and simple was the device employed in 1934 by a Bombay rogue named Purshotamdas Muni to acquire the wealth of the simple-minded.*

Ibid., 13 Nov., 1934

Posing as a mahatma, or saintly religious teacher, he gained admission to the household of one Kallianji Walji, a devout Hindu dealer in electrical goods. During his stay as a guest he gave religious discourses, which were well attended and which impressed both Kallianji and his wife Kasurbai; and among his followers was an aged Gujarathi woman named Chhaturbai Nensa.

Having gained the confidence of his little circle, Muni announced the forthcoming advent on earth of the king-god Ram Raj, prophesied that a son born of Kasurbai would occupy the throne at Delhi, foretold the collapse of all banks, and asked his followers to withdraw their cash from the banks and deposit it with him for safety. Anyone with more critical acumen than a religion-crazed Hindu would have demanded some details as to how, for instance, the British power was to be got rid of; why the king-god would not himself mount the throne; and why on earth the ancient Muhammedan seat of Delhi should be chosen, anyway! To minds hypnotized by a mahatma, however, such things do not occur; and Chhaturbai fell a ready victim to the "prophecies". She handed over to Muni all her jewels, worth nearly 2000 rupees, and 1000 rupees which she drew from the bank. Of course, with this and other hauls, he vanished. When caught, he had the dubious pleasure of spending seven months in a verminous Indian gaol awaiting trial, so the judge took this into account, and only gave him a day's imprisonment, but fined him heavily on three fraud charges.

The universal Indian belief in astrology is one of the most prolific causes of deception. An alleged astrologer named Pandlit Mayadhari, who had been reading other people's future with considerable advantage to himself but failed to read his own, was given nine months hard labour at Amritsar in 1934. The bizarre story told in court* was that a villager, Mahaditta, worried over domestic trouble, consulted the Pandit about his horoscope. The astrologer undertook to consult the gods if Mahaditta would bring twenty-seven tolas of gold (worth about £70), which, he said, would be thrown into the river.

Times of India, 30 June, 1934

The poor peasant pooled all the jewelry in his home, but could muster only some fourteen tolas in gold-weight, which he took to the astrologer, who said it would have to suffice, and the pair took the train for an "auspicious spot" on the River Beas, after Mayadhari had apparently put the gold into a dumpling of flour, the idea being to throw this into the river as an offering, with incantations. On the journey, however, Mahaditta became suspicious, and wanted to make sure his gold was there, but the astrologer refused to let him see it, whereupon the peasant seized the ball of flour by force, broke it open, and found it stuffed with bits of old iron. He raised the alarm, pulling the communication-cord, and the Pandit was handed over by the railway guard to the police, who found the gold in his house.

The greatest and most audacious mass-ramp that came within my experience in India occurred in Bombay during the same year*, when the police rounded up nine out of a gang of twenty men, alleged to have used magic, drugging, and sorcery in systematic cheating for nearly two years. The chief of the gang was a *bhagat* (sorcerer), who played on the fears and superstitions of millhands, gardeners, and others of low intelligence. Selecting a victim, an accomplice would approach him on his way to work, stating that he (the accomplice) and his associates had secured a contract for building-construction which would earn them thousands of rupees. The only snag was that they had to find a small sum of money, some 200 rupees, to be deposited with the landlord to enable them to draw the sum contracted for. In return for providing the deposit money the victim was offered a partnership in the contract.

Evening News of India, 24 Dec, 1934

If the victim showed any reluctance, the swindler would express his regret that both of them would lose so golden an opportunity, and depart sadly; but the victim, going on his way, would be met further along the road by the *bhagat*, accosting him with the news that he would shortly be rich. There was nothing suspicious in this: in India these wandering sorcerers and "holy-men" frequently accost one in the street with news as to one's future. One told me, quite gratuitously, that I was due to be run over by a car in Bombay, and should never leave India.

Meanwhile, the *bhagat's* next accomplice comes up, in time to hear the prophecy; he questions the sorcerer's powers, whereupon the latter pretends to be deeply offended, and, muttering dire spells, apparently casts the accomplice into a trance. He then stresses that what he has foretold will assuredly happen. "I further read," says the seer, "that you have had an offer. You would do well to accept it."

The victim's doubts are now silenced, and when he has had time to think things over he is again "accidentally" met by the man who first accosted him, and eagerly makes an appointment to meet this and other members of the gang; they take him to a part of Bombay where building operations are in progress—there is always plenty of this in the city. He is relieved of his "deposit-money", and the gang, on pretext of going to pay it to the landlord, enter one of the buildings and vanish out of the back door before the victim has time to recover the few wits he possesses.

Another ingenious scheme employed by this gang was worked on rich invalids. Getting an introduction to a selected victim, a member of the gang would declare that his illness was the work of an evil spirit and that it could be exorcized by a *bhagat*. The victim agreeing, our sorcerer turned up on an appointed day with a disciple and, after performing *puja* (rites of worship), offered the invalid and his family alleged holy water from the Ganges. The water, of course, was doped; the inmates of the house fell unconscious, and the gang cleared the place of all portable valuables. In one case, so potent was the drug that the gang narrowly escaped a charge of murder, for the invalid was saved only with difficulty.

Sometimes duping by Indian knaves is carried too far, and actually does end in tragedy, and a charge far more serious than that of fraud. One such case I recall was in the State of Hyderabad,* where a villager died in hospital after an operation which revealed that he had been forced to swallow 105 copper coins and a quantity of hot green chilies. Death came to him thus horribly as the penalty of his swindling schemes.

*Evening News of India, 29 May, 1934.

This man had convinced a Marwari acquaintance that he possessed occult powers whereby he could double the amount of money and ornaments. So well did he "tell the tale" that not only this Marwari but also three others handed over jewels, worth in all some 5000 rupees, for a demonstration. The "magician" buried them in a wooden box, at a spot known to all the men, and performed *puja*, warning the Marwaris that they must not, for fear of breaking the spell, attempt to dig up the box before three months had elapsed, at the end of which time they would find double the amount of jewelry they had buried. When the great day came, they naturally found in the box only stones and a few copper pice; their sorcerer was evidently an expert at sleight-of-hand.

Keeping quiet about the affair for fear of public ridicule, the Marwaris swore revenge, combed the whole of Hyderabad State for the man, found him, and forcibly took him back to the scene of the swindle. Here they bound him hand and foot and, it was alleged, made him swallow the chillies and 105 half-anna coins. When set free, he had only enough strength left to stagger to the nearest police station and gasp out his tale. Only one of the four Marwaris was caught, and he was charged with culpable homicide. The papers failed to record the result of the case.

Chapter 3

Crime and Sorcery

CRIME, religious belief; and magic are entangled together in Indian life to a degree absolutely inconceivable to the western mind; a man thinks nothing, for instance, of trying to obtain the aid of his deity in hushing-up a murder. We had a good instance of this at Ratnagiri in 1933, where the bizarre circumstances lent interest to an otherwise commonplace and 'sordid story of illicit passion and murder.*

*Times of India. 18 July, 1933

A peasant from a village of the district was on trial for the murder of a man with whose wife he was alleged to be on adulterous terms, and for robbing the man's house into the bargain. Among the prosecution witnesses was the priest of the village temple, who said the prisoner visited the temple and actually asked him to offer prayers to the goddess to secure her aid in getting the murder hushed-up, promising a reward of gold in return for the service.

The same town was the scene only six months later of an amazing court story of how one man believed another had sent an evil spirit to trouble him, obtained from the god of his village an oracular sign confirming that belief, and was alleged to have forthwith murdered the supposed worker of spells.*

*Evening News of India, 23 Feb., 1934

The victim was a rich landlord, and the accused was a peasant. In this case also a temple priest was called as witness, and he stoutly maintained that the village god did give the peasant a sign (though unfortunately for occult science he omitted to describe the nature of it) confirming that the landlord had sent the evil spirit; and another witness corroborated this miracle. Up to this point the story reads like an English witch-trial of the seventeenth century, but then transpires the prosaic information that the landlord had obtained a decree evicting the peasant from his farm-holding, which provided a mundane motive for the alleged crime.

About the same time as the first case we have quoted there was one before the sessions at Nagpur* in which a man was charged with murdering his neighbour, who, he alleged, had put the evil eye on his wife, causing her to be ill. This, of course, comes more strictly under the heading of ordinary witchcraft, while the first two cases strikingly demonstrate the widespread belief in the magical power of images, a subject we shall examine in another chapter.

*Times of India, 29 June, 1933

In such terror does the Indian hold even a mere threat to conjure a demon that he who utters it not infrequently loses his life. In one such case, in Patiala State, two Harijans, or members of the Depressed Classes (the casteless pariahs of Indian society), were quarrelling, when one threatened to cause a demon to enter into the son of the other. The latter decided that the only way to lay the demon was to lay low the threatener, which he did with a knife. He then went and confessed to the police, saying he committed the murder to save the life of his son.*

*Evening News of India, 2 June, 1934

The wild jungles of Hyderabad State provided a weird court story of a plot to do away with a police Patel (district head constable), in which both magic, bizarre jungle ritual, and mundane cheating, figured.* Four villagers wished to get rid of the police officer, against whom they had a grudge, so they applied to a notorious sorcerer of the district, who consented to "eliminate" the unfortunate officer by magic, if the four clients would meet him in the jungle by moonlight, bringing with them 300 rupees, his fee. He also gave them a lime, which he said they must bury in the compound of the officer's house—the burial of an object near the victim is a common feature of sympathetic magic the world over.

*Evening News of India, 10 April, 1934

The men managed to scrape together the cash, and buried the lime fruit.

In the jungle clearing, the sorcerer made the four men sit at the corners of a square, lit fires all round them, and chanted spells. He then gave them toddy to drink, saying it would protect them from the evil spirit which would kill the police officer the moment their incantations were finished. The toddy was doped with dhatura poison, and the sorcerer was able to make off with the men's money, leaving them in a state of stupor. Curiously enough, the affair only came to light when a *dhobi* (washerman) employed by the Patel, who had helped the conspirators bury the lime in his master's courtyard, committed suicide in a well, fearing the vengeance of the gods.

For a story of black magic run riot and ending in murder, however, I have never met with any case to excel a trial that opened in April 1934 at Nasik, the most holy (and, as a natural corollary, the filthiest) "city" of western India.* In the dock stood Raniji Balm Warli, charged with the murder of a widow named Chimi, who was undoubtedly the victim of the man's belief that she was the cause of his domestic troubles, and that she had put a spell upon him by black magic; and the case illustrates the old proverb about the fury of a woman scorned.

Times of India, and vernacular press, 11 April, 1934

The trouble started with Chimi, a brazen young thing (as many girl-widows are in northern India), proposing that she should become Warli's mistress, an idea he rejected with horror. As she continued to pester him, coming to his hut and stripping herself naked, he threatened to report the matter to the police. She retorted with the threat, "If you do, I shall harm you," and to avoid her attentions he left the village. Soon after this one misfortune after another overtook him. His first and second children died in rapid succession; within a few days he lost his brother; three of his bullocks and two cows died mysteriously, and his crops were blighted.

In despair Warli took the only course he could think of: he consulted the *bhagat*, who strongly suspected that the "woman scorned" was responsible for this trail of misery. Warli, on his advice, got in touch with a renowned witch-doctor, who soon got busy on the grain-threshing floor with magical preparations. Putting a sour lime into a small bowl, he sprinkled *gulal*, a red powder, over it, and chanted incantations and mantras to a deity. The wizard then directed his assistant to hold his left hand just above the bowl and follow it.

Then, Warli told the court, an incredible thing happened. The bowl left the floor and began to move through the air of its own volition. First it went to the shrine of the village god in the temple, and after stopping there

33

awhile continued its uncanny progress. The witch-doctor remained behind, and Warli and the assistant followed the bowl, which travelled for nearly two miles, near the ground, until it reached the house of the woman Chimi, when it refused to move further. Chimi was at home. Warli and the assistant then returned to the witch-doctor, still waiting at the former's house, and he declared that Chimi was the witch who had caused all the trouble.

Soon after this Warli's wife died, his crops failed, and he was a ruined man. He fell ill, and every night saw a phantom ride though the air and sit on his chest. At last he could stand it no longer, so on 14 December, 1933, after harvesting, he took his scythe, sought out Chimi, and demanded point-blank to know who had been persecuting him with curses for the past three years. She angrily replied that if he tried to find out she would "utterly destroy him and his household". This was the last straw, and Warli lashed out with his scythe, killing the woman. He then went to the police, stating that he had not meant to commit murder, but his sufferings made him lose his self-control. Sentencing Warli to death, the judge remarked that his confession and remorse were no excuse for the crime, "especially when crimes impelled by superstition are common in this district", but he recommended the poor wretch to mercy.

The judge, by his remarks, seems to have thought the crime due to mere "superstition"—but when I was staying in the hinterland of Goa, almost the last remains of the great Portuguese Indian empire, my host, Senhor Francisco Rodrigues, chief landowner of the village of Curtorina, showed me extraordinary evidence, in a neighbouring jungle village, as to the power of a curse. He pointed out one of the largest houses, crumbling to decay, the compound of which looked as though every tree in it had been blasted by lightning, while on either side of it were compounds luxuriant with fertile coco-palms and mango-trees.

Then, about a mile away, he showed me holdings of palms and paddy-fields, equally stricken in appearance, right in the middle of fertile belts belonging to himself and his neighbours; and this is the story he told, on the authority of village tradition, to account for it. The great residence and lands, equivalent to an English manorial property, belonged to an ancient family of *descendantes*, landowners of mixed Portuguese and Indian descent, whose head, nearly a century ago, was notorious for his brutality, greed, and harshness to his tenants. The whole village got together and enlisted the aid of the witch-doctor who cursed the family in the following terms: The landowner should die by his own hand, nothing his descendants did should prosper; no land of theirs, or any they sold, should ever thenceforth be fertile; and the family should die out within a hundred years in poverty and insanity.

The reader may hold what opinion he chooses as to the power of curses, but the fact remains that in 1934 the last remnants of that family were the feebleminded old mistress of a manor-house mumbling about her fears, and her imbecile son, living in dire poverty; and that their compound, and the patches of land and palm-grove sold by them and their predecessors for two generations, lay utterly barren in the midst of abundant fertility, for no reason scientifically explicable.

It is not uncommon in India to find a god blamed for murder. One such case I recall was at Allahabad, where a man named Nar Singh was sentenced to death, but reprieved, for killing one Kalu Singh with an axe. When two of Nar Singh's children died, he thought Kalu had invoked a god against him, and that the deity was thus jointly responsible. A soothsayer whom he consulted agreed with this theory, and went so far as to declare his belief before the *panchayet*, or village council of elders, two days before the murder.*

Newspapers of 17 July, 1934

An even brighter idea prevails among the Kallan tribe of Madura, who are mostly professional robbers. If the road to a thieving expedition passes the shrine of a strange deity, they enter the temple and take the god into their confidence, promising him a sacrifice, or a percentage of the spoils, if he does not interfere with the enterprise; and they always keep their promise, returning after the raid. Before the offering is made, the god tells the *dacoits*, through the medium of his priest, exactly what they did at the robbery. This is easy, as such forays are always identical in procedure. The god then says he is willing to accept the gift, which is nearly always money or a goat.*

Miles, A., Land of the Lingam (1933)

From such a proceeding to the actual deification of a *dacoit* is not a very far cry, and investigations show that there are cases of the latter actually occurring. For instance, among the minor godlings of South Bihar are two, Goraiya and Salesh, which are frankly admitted by their worshippers to be the deified spirits of two ancient *dacoits* who appear to have played a kind of Robin Hood role, robbing the rich to aid the poor. The same tribe-group has another godling, Sokha Baba, who turns out to have actually lived as a very skilful doctor.*

Information from Mr. Sarat Chandra Mitra

Being a sorcerer is in India a profitable, but often a very hazardous, occupation, and almost every week one reads in the papers cases of alleged magicians losing their lives. Early in 1935 a sensational story of double murder was revealed in court at Broach, where a man was charged with killing his two cousins, whom he suspected of having directed against him *muth*, the Indian equivalent of voodoo.* The only feature at all out of the common in this case was the accused's evidence that he had been to a native doctor, who had tried to cure him of illness by tying a charmed thread round his arm, and endeavoured to get rid of his evil spirit by means of spells conducted with the aid of the time-honoured broomstick.

Times of India, 21 Jan. 1935

Out of hundreds of records of such cases we need only cite a few more. One is of interest as illustrating the deep dread of witchcraft in which live the primitive Dravidian tribal group known as the Khonds, whose sacrificial practices are described in our next chapter. The Madras police reports record that in the Vizagapatam hill district the youngest of three Khond brothers died of fever; when the body was cremated the upper part would not burn, so his brothers held that the death had been caused by the witchcraft of a man of the community. This individual they killed; they cut the body across into two halves and took the upper portion to their village, throwing it on the spot where their brother's corpse had refused to burn. The men were arrested and sentenced to death.

Even in the "civilized" environs of Bombay, fatal cases of violence from the fear of witchcraft occur. Thus "a carpenter named Govind, belonging to the village of Borivli, only fifteen miles out of the city, was "taken for a ride", beaten up, and murdered in the approved American manner, because he was held to have caused the death of a neighbour by black magic.*

Evening News of India, 11 July, 19344

Another case was that of a man of the Pannan caste, who was one morning found dead on a hillock in the Malabar village of Mandaka-Pallipuram. Five Moplahs (Malabar Muslims) and two Hindus were arrested in July 1934 in connection with the death; the only motive discoverable was that the man was much feared as an Odiyan, the Malabar term for a sorcerer, and was reputedly able to change into the shape of a cat or dog, in which guise he prowled round his enemies' houses at night.* We shall have more to say of the Odiyans a little later.

* *Times of India, 3 July, 1934*

Although the widespread terror of superstition has caused Indian jurists to insert in the penal code a section (508) whereby it is an offence to "induce a person to believe that he will become the object of divine "displeasure", to give its exact wording, this does not always provide complete protection. Thus there were two cases at Sinnar within a year, both brought under this section. In the first, which also involved a complaint of house trespass as the result of the trouble, two men forced their way into the house of the complainant, a woman, alleged that she was a witch, accused her of having "possessed" them, and demanded that she remove the spell.*

Ibid., and vernacular press, 24 June, 1933

They did a hideous dance, acted as though under demoniac possession, threatened that unless the woman broke the spell they would devour her, and finally pulled her hair, beat her, stripped off her bodice, and danced on her breasts. Naturally, she went to the police after all that ill-usage. In the second case, in the same town, a woman accused a villager, his daughter-in-law, his son, and two other men of calling her a witch and of alleging that she had caused her own daughter, who was a congenital idiot, to be possessed by an evil spirit. In this case the affair led to a hearty family brawl, which was finally dealt with under the mundane charge of rioting.*

Times of India, 15 May, 1934

A riot on a larger scale, also caused by a belief in magic, occurred at Ambali, a village of Borsad district, when the caste Hindus got the idea that an epidemic among the cattle was caused by the sorcery of the local outcastes, or Harijans, and demanded that they stop the magic. The Harijans caustically retorted that the disease would cease if the caste Hindus were clean, and the result was a pitched battle with the long Indian bamboo staves known as *lathis*.*

Ibid., 6 Aug., 1934

The Sinnar "witches" got off lightly. I heard of a case in Gujerat in which a suspected witch was stripped naked and spread-eagled over a fire, in which chillies and other pungent substances were put, to see if she were affected by the smoke. This is very reminiscent of our own barbarous English ordeal by swimming, which persisted right down to the early years of last century, the last recorded case of English witch-ducking not occurring till so late as 1813, when an old woman of Wellingborough was the victim.

The witch of India seems in attributes very much like her western counterpart. Sir Herbert Emerson, Governor of the Punjab, who takes a more intelligent interest in Indian customs and beliefs than most English officials, told the Lahore Rotary Club in 1935 the story of a famous witch of the river Sutlej, who had very long claws. This witch wanted to join a party on the far side of the river, who seemed to be throwing choice bits of food about. There was no bridge or boat, but she had a bright idea: there was a large rock on the opposite bank, so she shot out her great tongue till it reached the rock and walked across on it, presumably rolling up the tongue after her like a carpet. This story incidentally illustrates the widespread belief that things of evil cannot fly across a waterbarrier, but that is an aspect of folklore which is out of our context in this chapter.

Though hardly falling under the heading of serious crime and sorcery, a case from Secunderabad is worth recording here, because divination was involved, and combined with rough handling to lead to a court case. A Goanese, a Christian of sorts (being descended from the wholesale converts made at the point of the sword by the Portuguese), accused two lads of stealing his wristwatch. He took them to a house and there performed a very ancient Christian rite of divination, known as "Bible and key". This was employed so late as the 1840's in our English Midlands, but was there only used for the harmless purpose of finding out the initials of one's lover on Midsummer Eve and Hallowe'en. The Goanese used a pair of scissors instead of a key, suspended in the Bible by string, but the process was the same. He held it over a fire containing incense, muttering a number of names, and when he came to those of each of the two boys the Bible turned. He thereupon found them guilty, and caned them.*

Times of India, 16 June, 1934

An extraordinary affair, which incidentally shows the savage brutality too often exercised by the Indian native policeman, was reported from Katni, in which a woman and her daughter, members of the retrograde tribe known as the Ghonds (who are widely feared as magicians), nearly lost their lives through a belief in sorcery.*

*Ibid., 14 Dec., 1934

Being told that the death of his son and the illness of other members of his family were due to witchcraft, a local Muslim police sub-inspector, it was later alleged in court, summoned these two women to appear before him. His infant child died while they were there, whereupon his staff took the women to an empty room, stripped them stark naked and flogged them, made the mother drink water from a cesspit, and then, in turn—five men were concerned—raped the daughter. Accustomed as the Indian woman is to frequent and violent copulation, this was a bit too much, and the girl was dangerously ill as the result. So scandalous is the state of affairs in country districts that the native police managed to hush the matter up by their influence and the tenor in which they are always held, until rumours came to the ears of a European deputy inspector-general from Nagpur, who had the whole affair investigated and the men put on trial.

However brutal and damnable the action of the police sepoys in this particular case, their terror of witchcraft was not a blind, unreasoning fear, for the witchdoctors of India, known in different districts by various names, such as Bhagat, Ojha, Dugpa, and (in Malabar) Odiyan, are a very real cause of fear to the populace, and the methods they adopt to procure the gruesome materials for the working of their magic lead to the most revolting crimes.

The Odiyans, who take their names from *odi* (black magic), chiefly belong to out-caste sects living on the slopes of the Western Ghats, and they are fully conversant with the magical use of images to compass an enemy's death, or even to commit murder obligingly for a good client. Although we discuss the magic of images in another chapter, it is appropriate here to deal with the practices of the Odliyan. He makes a wooden image of the victim, drives nails into it, and burns it with special ceremonies and curses; and within the time prescribed the man dies, though he may not consciously know he has been bewitched. A variant of this is to bury a small frog, into the eyes of which nails have been driven, in an earthen pot covered by a new cloth; when it dies, the enemy also dies. This process is familiar to students of our English witch-trials, and even of harmless country leechcraft, a good instance of the latter being the belief that to cure a disease you must imprison a spider in a nutshell and put it in the chimney, whereupon the disease will abate as the spider dies.

When it is desired to inflict a punishment short of death, the Odiyan makes a series of mystic diagrams on a thin sheet of copper and buries it with incantations at a spot over which the victim is wont to pass, such as his own hut-threshold. On crossing it he crumples up and falls down, a cripple for life. I have met hardheaded Europeans who can vouch for this happening.

To accomplish his murders by sorcery the Odiyan first obtains a human foetus of seven months' growth.

He walks furtively at night round the hut of a woman in her first pregnancy, softly tinkling a low-toned bell and chanting mantras. Thus he casts the inmates into a deep sleep, and hypnotizes the woman into coming out of the hut, naked, in a state of trance. The sorcerer then forcibly removes the foetus from the poor wretch's body by making a few crude incisions in the womb; and many a woman has been found in Malabar outside her hut thus mutilated and dead from the ordeal. From the foetus the Odiyan extracts a magical oil, believed to give him the power of rendering himself invisible at will, or to take the shape of any animal he desires, the favourite shapes being of a dog, cat, or bull. We have seen how a man was murdered under suspicion of practising this sorcery.

The idea of magical properties inherent in the human foetus if obtained prenatally is probably connected with the conception among the primitive races that the female vagina, rather than the male organ, is the actual "giver of life",* the theory that the foetus must be seized and infused with the magician's personality before it acquires by normal birth its distinctive personality in this world.

*See Perry, W. J., Origin of Magic and Religion (London, 1923)

It is rather strange to find that less than forty years ago the older generation of English sailors still believed that the caul, a membrane which covers the beads of some infants at birth, and is rare to obtain, was an infallible charm against drowning; and they would often pay a high price for one.* In European magic I have rarely encountered a record of obtaining a prenatal foetus, though allegations of the murder of newborn children are common enough in its historical trial-records.

* Folklore county vols, Leicestershire (1894), p. 62.

The belief in the efficacy of homeopathic magic worked in the cause of crime by means of the dead or the unborn is very widespread, the object being to cast into deep sleep the inmates of a house to be burgled. Thus south Indian robbers will sprinkle ashes from a funeral pyre on their victim's doorstep; in Europe we had the famous Hand of Glory, a torch made from the withered hand of a malefactor who had died on the gallows; in the seventeenth century it was believed that the thief's candle should be made from a finger of a newborn child, or, better still, one unborn, and the robbers therefore murdered pregnant women to obtain from their wombs this material.* We thus gain some light on the reason for the Odiyan's practices.

*Frazer, J. G., The Golden Bough (Abridged edn., 1924),pp. 30-31

In India, to this day, the quest by sorcerers for the body of a newborn infant is a frequent source of child-disappearance and murder. In September 1934 there was a case* at Nayyattinkara, Travancore, where an Odiyan, who had promised certain men powers that would enable them to render people senseless and rob them, told his assistants to procure a child just born, so that it could be sacrificed and its brain used to prepare a potent drug. The man who tried to steal a child was caught in the act, and revealed the whole plot.

*Times of India, 21 Sept., 1914.

In the same part of India, earlier in the same year, an extraordinary story was told in court when a Syrian Christian (a misnomer, for the Christians of Cochin and Travancore are not Syrians, but Indian converts whose Christianity is a weird polyglot with Hinduism) was charged with roasting a baby for eight days in order to extract oil for the purpose of black magic."

This, it was alleged, he had actually done on the advice of a Christian priest, whom he consulted as to the best method of getting power to seduce a woman he wanted. It was never discovered whether the Christian and the two men who aided him actually killed the child or acquired a newly dead one; they told the magistrate that they took a dead body and, after roasting it for eight days, extracted a liquid substance from the head, and another from the trunk, which they put into separate bottles. These they hid in the earth, after throwing the roasting-pans into the river.

The past history of witchcraft, and practices elsewhere even today, show that very often in rites like this, a live body is deemed requisite. A terrible case occurred in the Borgville district of Natal, reported by Reuter and printed in the newspapers in July 1933, in which a witch-doctor cut off a hand, ear, and the private organs of a little child while still alive; and a few days later there came from Swazililand the report of a chief and four other men being sentenced to death for the ritual murder of an infant for the same purposes of black magic.*

Times of India, 18 Jan., 1934

Coming back to India, we had a case at Poona in November 1934 when a charge of murder and robbery was brought against several men alleged to nave killed a young girl-wife.* One, a rural herbal doctor, was stated to have told the others that if they provided him with the little toe of the left foot, the ribs, and a few locks of the hair of a young married girl, he would unearth buried treasure from the house of a certain woman. Later a young wife was missing from the village, and found to have been murdered.

Ibid., 7 Nov. 1934

While there is a class of men called Jaduwalas, which means "sellers of magic", who are more or less harmless quacks dispensing magical remedies for disease, love potions, and the like, these individuals learn much that is not so harmless from their teachers, the Dugpas, who may be described as master-magicians.

The Dugpa himself usually keeps in the background, and works through the Jaduwala as his emissary; but if there is lucrative inducement, he sometimes takes a hand in the devilry himself. The Hyderabad State police reports contain some very gruesome instances, and one may be quoted here as fairly representative.* The crime arose out of a rich woman's desire to appease evil spirits supposed to be guardians of treasure.

Hyderabad State Police Report for year 1333 fasli (A.D. 1926)

This woman, Radhama, asked a woman of the Kunbi (agriculturist) caste to procure for her a firstborn infant for the purpose of unearthing a treasure buried in her house, promising a reward for the service. Awaiting her opportunity, the Kunbi woman managed to kidnap the eighteen-months-old female child of a local goldsmith while it was playing in the street. She took the child to Radhama, who hid it in the upper storey of her house, giving the brat a strong dose of opium to keep it quiet. At night Radhama went to the spot where the treasure was supposed to be buried, accompanied by four men, three of whom dug while the fourth chanted mantras.

When the treasure had been found, the child was carried to the spot, brutally sacrificed to appease the guardian spirits, and buried in the hole from which the treasure had been taken. When the case ultimately came to light, the Nizam, after much legal argument, appointed a commission to inquire into it; but its findings are not known to the public. Enough came out, however, to show that this case was typical of the methods of the Dugpa; remaining in the background, the magician here concerned got his client, Radhama, to depute the Kunbi woman to procure the child, and he it was who suggested to the client the need for sacrifice.

A child-sacrifice is often performed for other reasons, such as a Dugpa's mere love of causing terror in his district; the appeasement of the wrath of the gods—an aspect of it with which I shall deal in the next chapter, as it more properly falls under the heading of religious human sacrifice—or the healing of an ailing person, which is invariably bound up with a belief in witchcraft causing illness, and which therefore comes into the category of crimes caused in connection with sorcery. I recall a case of this a few years ago in Hyderabad State, where a village woman was charged with murdering her own child. She was alleged in court to have sacrificed it to the local gods, on the advice of a witch, to cure a relative's illness. The woman was acquitted, however.

Cases of infanticide performed by barren women in the hope of securing children of their own are very frequent, and instances are recorded where the murderess bathed her own body in the still warm blood of her victim, in the hope that this would result in the rebirth of the dead child in her own womb—a most interesting illustration of the primitive belief in blood as the giver of life.

An illuminating case of human sacrifice to cure illness is recorded by Somerville* from Mandla, in the Central Provinces, where a whole family was put on trial in March 1925. According to the evidence, a government servant named Mulchand lived at Mandla with his family, consisting of three sons (Chotey Singh, Bhopat Singh, and Lukhman Singh), his daughter Rukbiman, and a daughter-in-law, Janki, wife of Bhopat Singh. In December 1924 Lukhman Singh, a mere boy, fell ill, and, medical treatment proving ineffective, the family believed the lad was possessed by an evil spirit and that human sacrifice was necessary.

*Somerville, A. (Crime and Religious Belief in India. Calcutta. 1931. 154 sqq.)

The woman Janki, it was alleged, first severed one of the girl Rukbiman's little fingertips and put some of the blood on a piece of bread, which was taken to a place where a certain holy man usually sat. Finally the girl was killed as a sacrifice to the goddess Kali, embodiment of the powers of darkness and divine vengeance.

When even this proved ineffective, the boy Lukhrnan Singh was starved and, despite the bitter cold, was taken naked, bound hand and foot, and deposited in the open near the spot where the holy man sat, in the hope that this would drive out the devil-but actually it caused the boy's death from exposure.

The other members of the family were arrested and tried on a charge of murder before four assessors (who in the Indian system function as a cross between a preliminary-trial jury and a bench of magistrates). The assessors found them not guilty, on the ground that although the boy died from cold and exposure, it was not intended to cause his death; and as regards the killing of the girl Rukbiman, they actually held that the guilt of the accused was excused, because they all believed that by this human sacrifice they were only obeying the dictates of a divine being! The sessions judge, to whom the case then went, rejected this view, but agreed with the assessors regarding the death of the boy, and he sentenced the family accordingly in the case of the girl.

Another case, also cited by Somerville,* came from Kishoreganj in May 1925, but, unfortunately, neither the motive for the murder nor the result of the trial is known. The newspapers said a report had reached the town that a twelve-year-old Sudra (servant-caste) boy was sacrificed before the image of Kali in a village three miles away on the previous Amavasya (full moon) day; his corpse, with flowers and betel-leaves on it, was found next morning under a tree.

*op. cit.

Sometimes death is caused through a belief not in sacrifice but in violent methods of leechcraft, and when this happens the plea, as in the Mandla case above, is one of "good faith". For instance, a woman charged at Nasik in 1934 with homicide as the result of the death of her daughter-in-law, Laxmi, told the court that she branded the girl with a red-hot implement because it was a very effective cure for many ailments, including the kidney disease from which the poor wretch was suffering. She said she had first obtained the girl's consent to the branding.*

*Evening News of India, 10 May, 1934 -62

Even the expert exorcist sometimes overdoes his treatment; in a Calcutta case, which happily did not end fatally, an Ojha was called in to drive out the evil spirit believed to be possessing a young Bengali mother, who, a few days after giving birth, developed signs of mental aberration. The magician arrived at the house with a weird assortment of animal skeletons and other charms, which he spread on the floor, reciting spells. He then put a piece of camphor on the palm of the girl's hand and set fire to it, ignited some cotton said to be Brahmin sacred thread in the flame, and pressed it to the lips of the patient. As we may expect, the poor girl was rather badly burnt, and had to be rushed to hospital; but the Ojha was very disappointed, and declared that she was not possessed of an evil spirit, because if she had been she would have remained untouched by the fire. The man was detained by the police on a charge equivalent to "causing grievous bodily harm".*

*Times of India, 22 Nov., 1934.

While the branding in this incident was purely superstitious, the Nasik woman who accidentally killed her patient at least had the sanction of oriental medical practice, for branding was formerly widely resorted to in India for the cure of jaundice. Moreover, it is not unknown in our own old English leechcraft; until the development of, modern veterinary science it was common in the Midlands to brand cattle to cure the disease known as blackleg. They were branded through the ear or dewlap, usually on the first Friday after the birth of the calf found suffering from the complaint. Evans, the great Midland authority on folk-customs, tells us* that by 1880 the practice had almost died out. Comparable with it was the custom of driving cattle through "need-fires", or the smoke of them, as a charm in time of cattle plague, for which there was probably a scientific basis, if the smoke acted as a germicide.

*Leicesiershire Words, Phrases and Proverbs (1880), s.v. "blackleg"

The dreaded Odiyan of Malabar is an expert exorcist, and this is almost his only function beneficial to his fellows. The Odiyans hold that an evil spirit possessing a person can be made to leave him, enter the magician, and drink blood; so the Odiyan, after doing a devil-dance, bites the necks of many live fowls, or a sheep, and sucks the blood, to achieve the transference of evil.

The most elaborate of his rites, however, involves self-torture. Driving into a Malabar village one day I was greeted by a most unearthly din of drums and trumpets, as though the whole place was going mad in some festival *tamasha*, and my anthropologist's curiosity was aroused, as it was not the season of any usual festival. I was told a particularly malevolent brand of evil spirit had taken possession of three men, and even sent some of the cattle mad, and I was just in time to see the beginning of the hired Odiyan's performance.

Driving a knife into his arm, he smeared his face with the warm blood. He was then swathed in a kind of winding-sheet, to incantations and a long, low note from the trumpets, and lowered into a grave, which was filled up. I was told that several hours later he would be exhumed and brought out of his cataleptic trance by a blare of alleged music, and that thereupon the spell would be broken. The idea, of course, was that by the transference of the evil spirit to his own body, attracted thither by the blood he had drunk, and the sympathetic-magic process of counterfeiting the death and burial of that body, the spirit would be "killed" and buried in the earth. Apparently for the same reason of blood attraction, the Odiyan, when called upon to exorcize a village from an epidemic, slashes his head with sacrificial knives, and in addition frightens off the disease demon by a terrific noise with drums and bells.

The Badagas, an agricultural caste of the Talamalai hills, live in constant terror of the witch-doctor and his power to open all locks and bolts by magic, as is the case with the Malabari Odiyan. The usual purpose of the Badaga sorcerer's housebreaking, however, is less fiendish than that of the Odiyan; it is merely to ravish the women, who, owing to the subtle quality of the magic, and the invisibility of the Badaga wizard, do not know they have been ravished! This, of course, is a very good excuse if the results of misconduct become evident some months later; and as for the girl's ignorance of what has happened, well, one sarcastic old Badaga told me that the women "do it so often that they don't feel the difference"!

The Badaga caste employ the services of the sorcerer when any member of the family is suffering from the evil eye, or demoniac possession. If they get the idea that the witch-man is playing into the hands of the demon, and not trying to remove it, they set upon him and subject him to a kind of ordeal by battle. Every Badaga family pays a yearly "subscription" to the dreaded necromancer, and woe betide anyone who forgets, or is not generous enough, for then spells fall thick and fast upon him.

One very excellent way to get rid of a demon appears to be by competition! The Pazhur Kaniyans of Travancore, who, in addition to being a famous caste of astrologers, are practitioners of sorcery and exorcism, achieve this by sending several of their number to the house of a person possessed of a spirit, disguised as still more fearsome demons, and perform a devil-dance before the house, whereupon the original demon departs in a great fright. The homeopathic reasoning which lies behind this is undoubtedly the same as that which impelled our ancestors to carve the nightmare forms of their gargoyles to keep evil spirits out of the churches in medieval Europe.

The greatest experts in this class of exorcism, however, are the medicine-men of Ceylon, in their capacity of devil-dancers. The masks they use when dancing in a frenzy as demons to drive out the evil spirit possessing a sick man are the weirdest in the world, and the Cambridge artist, Justin Pieris, who returned to England in 1935 after risking his life to paint and collect these masks in the depths of the Sinhalese jungle, tells strange stories of the power of these men. He relates* how one of them, walking along the street, was stumbled against by a man who, instead of apologizing, uttered an insult. The medicine-man merely smiled, and said: "You may need me tonight, my friend. You had better take my address." That same night the man was taken violently ill and, remembering the old man's words, sent for him, a distance of some ten miles. When the medicine-man arrived the man who had offended him was writhing in the grip of a terrible fever; but the witch-doctor refused to lift a finger to save him, and stood smiling while he died.

*The People, 28 July, 1935

The Travancore Kaniyans, in addition to their devil-dancing, claim to cure disease by a process well known in sympathetic magic. They cut a rope the length of the sick person, which is a variation of making an image; they then make knots in it, presumably to tangle up the demon when it leaves the patient and enters the rope, and pass it several times through the smoke from burning goat-hair on which drops of blood from a sacrificed chicken have been sprinkled. I have never been able to discover why goat hair is so favoured in this and other fumigation rituals, and the magicians themselves frankly admit they do not know; but I would suggest that its origin lies in the goat being a milk-giver, and therefore a magical surrogate of the cow, the universal symbol of life-giving and the mother-goddess in early culture. However, the mention of a slaughtered chicken brings us now to that great and dark feature of Hindu ritual, human and animal sacrifice.

Chapter 4

Human Sacrifice

ENGLISH officials in India often complacently state that British rule has wiped out both human sacrifice and *sati* (suttee), the practice of self-immolation by a widow on her husband's funeral pyre, but cases of the latter persistently occur, and the former also goes on to an extent not often realized. The ultimate abolition of both would have to come from within Hinduism itself if at all; the plain truth is that the English are thoroughly detested in India, and all attempts to interfere with basic practices of the Hindu's faith only deepen the hatred and drive those rites underground.

The problem of human sacrifice cannot logically be regarded with the Anglo-Saxon eye, which looks upon all taking of human life as a crime. Western science does not, and never will, know what power the ancient earth-forces may possess, and is not entitled to declare that the sacrifice of a victim does not, for instance, terminate a drought. The western administrator has, therefore, no moral right to interfere; and every sentence imposed upon those concerned in ritual sacrifice only increases the Hindu's hatred. The western mind cannot possibly conceive the intense belief the Hindu holds, that the very stability of the universe depends on the regularity of sacrifice, since the gods live upon the spiritual portion of the victim. This is just as reasonable to the Hindu as the doctrine that the bread and wine in the Mass become the body and blood of Christ is to the Catholic. Who shall say with proof that either belief is untenable?

As a proof that if the concepts of Hinduism alter, relevant practices may also alter, we may cite the case of *sati*. This is chiefly prevalent in northern India and Bengal, where the lot of the Hindu widow is so miserable as to be practically a living death; it is very rarely heard of in south India, where there is widespread matriarchy, and where, for the most part, the widow has her independence and the right to remarry.

The latest case of human sacrifice on record has occurred as I write this chapter, at Gunpur, in Nahan district, where five men have just been sentenced to long terms of imprisonment in connection with it.* To end a drought, which caused great distress in the village, the priest advised a human sacrifice to the rain-god. A young man of twenty-three was decoyed from a neighbouring village by the headman, kept in chains in a locked room for three days without food or water, then led through the village street in chains, garlanded, his forehead smeared with vermilion and ashes, and finally beheaded in front of the temple. His wife committed suicide at the police-station when informed of his death.

The People, 9 Jan., 1938

The reasons for which human sacrifice is committed in India are highly instructive to the anthropologist, going back far beyond the present elaborate structure of Hinduism; hence, the only grounds upon which the scientific mind can condemn the practice is not because it is any "crime", but merely that it belongs to the most primitive stratum of cultural belief, and that Hinduism would, by abolishing it, become more enlightened intellectually. The basic origin of the rite, as Frazer has shown very fully,* lies in the widespread agricultural ritual of the earliest Mediterranean culture, in which the king was actually killed after a certain term, or when he became old and feeble, so that the life of his community and the fertility of the crops, held to be bound up with the living person of the priest-god-king, should not die.

The Golden Bough, passim

Striking proof of this has been found in the seventy wholesale royal burial pits discovered by Woolley at Ur, and there is evidence that this early culture spread eastwards from its original home in the Nile valley*

See Perry, Origin of Magic and Religion

Later, a scapegoat for the king in the person of a sacrificed human subject, was substituted, his blood ensuring by proxy the fertility of the crops, and in Egypt particularly the regular recurrence of the inundation; and further afield, the necessary rains. On a further extension of the original concept, coming with the later development of the idea of individual deities, we find human sacrifice applied for the appeasement of the gods and goddesses of disease.

The connection of kingship and tribal life in the early ritual is well illustrated by the practice of the Naga tribal group living in Manipur, Assam. Hodson* states that among these Nagas "a chief's funeral is incomplete without the head of a human victim, and he suggests that the victim is killed by the community as a solemn communal act, so that it may get power over, and, as it were, retain possession of the great man who has been reft from the tribe."

*Hodson, W. C.. The Naga Tribes of Manipu

For this purpose head-hunting prevails among the Nagas of the southern portion of the unadministered territory west of the Hukwang river. In the northern part of that territory, however, they do not go head-hunting, but buy or kidnap a victim for the sacrifice. When they purchase one he is apparently obtained from the headhunting Nagas, the price being about 500 rupees (£40).

For a fortnight before the date of the sacrifice the victim is stupefied with drink; then on the great day he is led to the top of the steps of the officiant's house and his head is cut off. The blood, spouting down the steps, is held to keep away evil spirits from the house. The body is then cut into pieces, which are hung up in houses at the entrance to the village, at crossroads (a spot universally feared as a haunt of evil), and in the fields, to ward off blight and to ensure good crops.

The same agricultural background is seen in most of the Indian rites of *meriah*, as the human sacrifice ritual is called. One of the Bengal castes practises it quite avowedly to ensure abundant crops, declaring that human blood is the only thing that will increase the harvest.* The offering is made to the earth-goddess, here called Tan Pennu, and the victim will not be "recognized" by the goddess unless he is born in the subdivision of the caste particularly earmarked for sacrifice. The victim in this case is held most holy, as by his death he benefits all mankind. In this he most strikingly resembles Osiris and Tammuz in their function of the dying but free-living redeemer-god, from which originated the Christian legend of the sacrifice of Jesus as saviour, an inescapable fact, however little the devout Christian may like to stomach the statement.

*Miles, A, The Land of the Lingam, 25 sqq.

Certain of the consecrated victims-to-be among the Tan Pen worshippers are kept for years before they are sacrificed, and are treated with all honour. Until the appointed time for his fate, a victim's hair is allowed to grow; it is then shorn and distributed to the people, who plant it with their seeds. The significance of this is obvious.

Wild debauchery precedes the final rites. The victim, dressed in a new garment, is paraded before the devotees and taken to the spot in the jungle chosen for the sacrifice. He is tied to a tree and anointed with *ghi* (clarified butter), turmeric, and flowers. The use of the turmeric, or sail-on, paste is a little obscure, but it figures so widely in Indian ceremonies that there can be little doubt that it is a much-distorted surrogate of a "giver of life" in the early magico-religious ritual, possibly by association of its colour with gold. This is a very complicated subject, for which the reader had best refer to Perry's illuminating *Migrations of Early Culture.*

Anything taken from the victim at this time is sacred. The worshippers* almost suffocate him as they close in and try to get a drop of his spittle to rub on their hair, or a smear of the turmeric to rub on their bodies. Prayers are addressed to the earth goddess, and a very primitive earth-dance is performed.

I am indebted to Miles, op. cit., for this description

This adoration of the saviour-victim lasts several days. On the final day he is again anointed with oil, and each member of the crowd rubs his hand on the oil and smears it on his own person. Then the victim is strangled, the usual mode of execution, though there are others.

At a sign from the officiant, each worshipper rushes up and tears from the victim's body a lump of flesh, which he will later throw on his fields to enrich the crops. The head and intestines must not be touched, otherwise the sacrifice will not be acceptable to the goddess. This is a somewhat unusual provision, as regards the head, for there is reason to believe that in the early world it was the head of the victim—in the first instance the feeble old king—that was thrown on the fields to ensure fertility. An undoubted survival of it is seen to this day in certain folk customs of England, notably the curious and famous ball-game known as Hasty Hood at Haxey in Lincolnshire, and the equally famous Bottle-kicking of Hallaton in Leicestershire.

In the old days, Miles states, the victim in the Bengal rite was cut up alive, and his flesh distributed among the caste, or he was slowly burned to death, when, the more he struggled and screamed, the more abundant would be the harvest. In the latter case the head and intestines were never given to the caste; they were burnt thee days after the sacrifice, and the ashes scattered on the fields or placed before the idol of the goddess.

In both methods we have the reservation of the intestines. This, combined with the complete resemblance of the victim to Osiris, seems to suggest a dim survival of the original Egyptian culture, since in Egypt the intestines were specially preserved and placed under the protection of certain guardian gods, one for the small and one for the large intestines, and placed with other organs in the so-called Canopic jars. There seems to be some idea with the Bengal caste that part of the personality of the saviour-victim must be thus preserved.

The fierce Khond tribes, whose chief centre is the Khond Hills, some 400 miles south of Calcutta, no longer dare to practise their *meriah* openly, but pretend to be content with sacrificing buffaloes, goats, and sheep since about 1870, before which time it was customary often to immolate three men at a tune on the altars of the earth-goddess, variously known as *Pan Pennu, Bera Pennu*, or, among the Maliah Khonds, *Thada Pennu*. One of the three victims was for the sun—the only instance of this that I can find in Indian records—another to the east end of the village, and the third to its west end, but all were really offerings to the earth mother.

In the *meriah* rite of the Khonds, a wooden post some six feet long, with a crossbar near the top, was sunk into the ground, and to it the sacrificial victim was tied by his long hair. A narrow grave was dug under the post, and four men held the arms and legs of the human offering, who was suspended horizontally over the grave. The officiating priest hacked pieces out of the victim's back while reciting a long invocation. The goddess was implored to eat the offering, and in return to give the Khonds swords and victory over other castes, and there was always a special prayer for the preservation of the caste from the tyranny of kings and governments.*

Miles, op. cit., 79—80.

The "scapegoat" significance of the ceremony is emphasized by the curious apology made to the victim, when almost cut to pieces, by the priest, saying: "Be not grieved, for the goddess will eat thee once. We bought thee from thy parents, who knew we intended to sacrifice thee, and therefore there is no sin on our heads, but on the heads of thy parents."

After this speech the priest decapitated the victim, the body rolled into the grave; and the head was left hanging on the post till the wild beasts and vultures devoured it, while the knife was stuck into the post and left until required for the two sacrifices that followed.

Frequently the victim was saved by the frenzy of the worshippers from being cut to pieces alive. They often surrounded him first, and killed him by beating his head with brass bangles made for the occasion, and if that did not kill him they finished him off by strangulation with a split bamboo, after which the priest cut up the body and distributed the fragments, with which the Khonds dashed off to the stream irrigating their fields, and hung the pieces of flesh on a pole over the water. The mangled remains of the corpse were finally buried with funeral obsequies, as the Khond does not burn his dead. It will be noticed that in the final address to the victim, stress is laid on his having been purchased, while we have seen that the person for sacrifice among the Nagas of Assam is sometimes bought. The idea of this seems to be that of removing the blood-guilt from the sacrificing tribe or *sept* by making the victim one not of its division. This is not always so, however; at the census of 1901 no fewer than twenty-five descendants of persons who had been reserved for sacrifice at a former Khond *meriah* rite, but who were "rescued" by government officials, returned themselves as *meriah*.

The agents sent to investigate *meriah* have left it on record, in the Vizagapatarn district manual, that there was reason to believe that a former Raja of Jeypore, when installed on the throne of his father, sacrificed a girl of thirteen to the goddess Durga, a form of Kali, who is herself the chief form of the earth-goddess, in the town of Jeypore. Several cases of human sacrifice, presumably to obtain victory, were discovered in the Rampa rebellion of 1880, and in the same year two persons were convicted of attempting to carry out *meriah* near Ambadala, in the district of Bissamkatak. Three years later a man was found murdered, in circumstances pointing to *meriah*, in a Jeypore temple; a formal inquiry in 1886 showed that there was reason to believe victims were being kidnapped for the rite in Bastar; and so recently as 1902 the district magistrate of Ganjam was openly confronted with a petition asking him to sanction a human sacrifice.

Female infanticide, Miles states,* was formerly so common in the Jeypore territory as to be farmed out as a paying business. The Raja himself is said to have made money out of it, thus: The custom was to consult the priest concerning the fate of the expected child before its birth. If he decided it was to be killed, the parents had to pay the headman of the caste division a fee for the privilege of killing it, and the headman paid the Raja a fee of 300 rupees a year for renting the privilege to perform these ritual killings. In connection with this, Macpherson has recorded that the area of the Khond country where female infanticide was known to prevail was about 2,000 square miles, that the population was about 64,000, and that some 1200 to 1500 infants were sacrificed annually.

Op. cit., 80-81

No light on the offering to the sun-god of the first of the three *meriah* victims is cast by the fact that certain divisions of the Khonds worship the sun-god, for these divisions make no sacrifices. The *septs* ,which practised female infanticide, however, believe that the sun-god deplores the birth of females, because the female creation has caused all the trouble in the world. Even these divisions, though, did not practise adult sacrifice. There seems scope here for some research, as it is generally conceded that the Khonds belong to the Dravidian stock; they are found scattered over Orissa, Bengal, Ganjam, and the Central Provinces, and are differently called, according to their district.

The Maliahs of Guinsur, who are also Khonds, sacrificed annually to the earth mother under the form of *Thada Pennu*. Several villages in a group would contribute to the purchase of a victim; no criminal or prisoner, and no victim who had not been fully paid for, was acceptable to the goddess, and grown men were most esteemed for sacrifice, because they were the most expensive.

When children were purchased for the purpose they were reared by the family who bought them, and were treated with kindness and honour till they grew old enough to know their fate, then they were guarded against escape. Finally, on the first day of the ceremonies, the victim was stupefied with toddy or opium, and seated, garlanded, against the *meriah*-post, while the worshippers danced round him chanting: "O Thada Pennu, we offer thee this sacrifice. Give us good crops and good health."

The victim was then dragged home; on the next day, having been again doped or intoxicated, he was anointed with oil, each worshipper touching the anointed part and rubbing the oil on his own body. The crowd then formed a procession round the village, carrying both the victim and the *meriah*-post, which had been dug from its hole and which was decorated with a tuft of peacock feathers at its top. When the procession returned to the *meriah* ground the priest cut a piece of flesh from the victim and buried it under the village idol. He then presented each of the villagers with a piece of flesh, with which they ran post-haste to their land, to bury it before sunset.

There was a peculiar end to this ceremony. After the human sacrifice, the priest and his men killed a pig and let its blood flow into the human victim's grave before burying him. On the next day a buffalo calf was taken to the post, to which it was tied, its forefeet were cut off, and it was left there till next day, when drunken women, in male attire and armed with sticks, danced and sang round the dying creature. It is difficult to see the significance of the pig in connection with the crop fertility ritual.

An interesting case of human sacrifice in which the victim's remains are not thrown on the land is that alleged still to be practised in secret by a hill-tribe near Vizagapatam, called Kotia Kudulu, whose offering is, however, known to be made to the god Jankari to secure good crops. The features of the actual ceremony correspond largely with those we have described: the man is bought, he is kept in a state of stupefaction, and is decorated with turmeric, but he is allowed complete liberty, even to the right of copulating with any woman he may meet while wandering about the village.

"On the day set apart for the sacrifice," states an English official who made a report on the matter, "he is carried before the idol in a state of intoxication. One of the villagers acts as priest, who (sic) cuts a small hole in the stomach of the victim, and with the blood that flows from the wound the idol is smeared. Then the crowds from the neighbouring villages rush forward, and he is literally cut into pieces. Each person who is so fortunate as to procure it carries away a morsel of flesh and presents it to the idol of his own village."

Some years ago an English Army officer stationed among the hill-tribes of Khondistan actually ordered his men to destroy the sacred effigies of elephants because human offerings had been made on them. The elephant in India is the symbol of the god Ganesh, or Ganpati. According to his account, the man to be sacrificed was tied to the trunk of the elephant effigy and whirled round until, at a given signal from the priest, the crowd rushed in with knives and chopped off all his flesh.

The Khonds' own legend of their origin is one of human sacrifice, and is a very interesting form of creation legend to the student of folklore.* In the beginning, it runs, when the earth was all wet, there were only two women living on it, each of whom had a son. They and their children came from the interior of the earth, bringing with them two plants which were their food. Cutting one of the plants one day, one of the women accidentally cut her finger, and the blood dropped to the ground, which at once became dry. Cooking the plant, the woman gave it to her son, who asked why it tasted so much sweeter than usual. She said she did not know, but expected to have a dream, and would tell him next day.

*Quoted by Miles, op. cit., 88-89 .76

As the result of the vision, she next morning made her son promise to do as she told him if he would prosper in the world. He must forget that she was his mother, and must cut the flesh from her back and bury it in the earth. This the son did, whereupon all the wet soil dried up and became hard, and the animals, birds, and trees, of the world came into existence. A partridge then scratched the ground , and millet and rice grew. Up to this point the story bears a suspicious resemblance to the germination of corn from the body of the dead king-god Osiris.

The two sons, the tale goes on, agreed that, as the sacrifice of the woman had brought forth abundance from the ground, they must sacrifice a human being once a year. Here a god named Bura Panu and his daughters appear on the scene, without explanation, as is usual in Indian mythology, and we find them living with the earthmen. Naturally, the god's daughters gave birth! When these children grew up there was a dispute as to which should be sacrificed, and as they could not decide the point, the fathers sacrificed a monkey instead:

This made the goddess of the earth very angry, and she at once demanded the sacrifice of a proper human victim. The two fathers, still unwilling to give up their own children, searched for ten years for a victim, finally finding one in the five-year-old son of a man who was persuaded to sell the lad for the purpose. Where these two human beings came from, or how they came to be on the earth, is left unexplained, with the usual inconsistency of Indian myth.

The boy was fettered to prevent his running away, toddy was made from grain, and a post was erected—the first meriah-post—at which a pig was sacrificed. Two days before being offered up, the boy was tied to the post, and on the night before his immolation the priest poked a stick into the earth until the earth-goddess answered; round the hole from which she had spoken, pieces of wood were arranged in crisscross fashion, and an egg placed on the structure. On the next day the boy was made to lie face downwards on the wood; pieces of flesh were then removed from his back and buried, thus creating the place of worship for the caste, while other portions were put into the ground near a drinking-well, to increase the water. The remains of the corpse were then burnt on the pile of wood, and on the next day a buffalo was sacrificed and a feast given.

Another community with a legend of human sacrifice is the labouring caste of Malas, whose story seems to be a garbled version of the biblical Red Sea myth and, indeed, as it does not seem very ancient, it may even owe its invention to contact with early Christian wanderers in south India. According to this legend, the Kapus and the Balijas were fleeing from the Muslim invaders, when they came to the Pannar river, then in flood. Their pursuers were on their heels; while they were debating what to do, a man named Mala offered up one of his children as a sacrifice to the river goddess Gauthi. The waters at once divided to let the fugitives cross in safety, and obligingly closed up again to obstruct the Muhammedan pursuers.

In addition to the original motive of crop fertility, there are two other, and, of course, later, motives for *meriah* in India: divination, and the appeasement of the disease-deities. For the former we may cite the instance of the Lambadis, the carter-caste found all over western and southern India, whose women never wash their bodies, and stink at a distance of several hundred yards if the wind is favourable. Formerly it was an open practice of the Lambadi, when starting out on a journey, to bury a child up to its neck in the ground and drive his bullocks over it, the thoroughness or otherwise of its trampling determining the success of the journey. In the old days the Lambadis and the Khonds were the people chiefly active in the business of stealing or buying human sacrificial victims.

As is the case all over India, the Lambadis have been reduced by the government ban to substituting animal sacrifice for human in such rites as are openly carried out. Thus, if they become ill, this caste believe they can avoid death by moving to another village, and they sacrifice a goat or chicken midway between the two places; sometimes it is buried alive, and formerly this was done with a human victim as the scapegoat of the disease-demon. He was interred up to the neck, and a crude lamp, formed of a hollowed lump of paste containing oil and four lighted wicks, was placed on his head, the plague-fleers dancing round him until he died.*

*Miles, op. cit., 168

Coming to the aspect of *meriah* as a talisman against disease, an Interesting case of this came to light in 1932, when a priest of a village in Coimbatore district was tried for murder after sacrificing his twelve-year-old son to appease the wrath of Kandi-amma, the goddess of disease, who insisted on a libation of blood. At the inquest the priest said that the *jagganaut* (the car-festival) had not been celebrated for two years, which provoked the wrath of the goddess, who threatened to wipe out the village in an epidemic unless she were appeased with human blood. She appeared to the priest in a vision, and told him only the blood of his own son could expiate the sin of failing to hold the car-ceremony; so he decapitated the boy with an axe and poured his blood out before the idol.* When one realizes how important a son is to a Brahmin, who is in danger of not reaching heaven unless the son carries out his obsequies, and when one knows the store which all Hindus set by the possession of a son, it is obvious that this was no case of wilful murder, and that the man should never have been placed in the dock.

*Miles, op. cit., 27.

Animal sacrifices in connection with disease, all of which have their origin in the offering of a human victim, will be dealt with in the next chapter. Before we leave the present aspect of the subject, however, there are a few miscellaneous instances of human sacrifice for reasons that fall under none of the headings we have been considering. A rather long-winded legend of the Palli caste, for example, relates how in the dim past the Palli *jagganaut* car was stuck fast owing to the spells of a rival caste of weavers, and how it could not be moved until one of the Pallis, a Prime Minister of a distant state, sacrificed his own pregnant wife and her unborn child to the goddess, as the result of her command in a vision.

Sometimes sacrificial infanticide has a most trivial and inexcusable motive. A few years ago a woman named Musammat Umrai, of Sujauli village, Lucknow, suddenly lost her voice while singing with other women. After consultation the women decided a sacrifice must be made to the goddess Bhagavati; whereupon Umrai decoyed a little girl named Kunia to a *nim-tree*, sacred to this goddess, felled her with a spade, and hacked the body to pieces. On trial, Umrai stated that this sacrifice was efficacious, all the women being able to sing much better after it, but that did not save her from the death sentence.

This provides an interesting instance, apparently, of human sacrifice in tree-spirit worship, the wide distribution of which is well attested. Originally the tree itself is looked upon as an animate thing; a later stage of belief is that it is the abode of a spirit; and later still comes the view that only certain species of trees have spirits dwelling in them. An example of this last is found in the Kangra Mountains of the Punjab, where a girl used to be sacrificed annually at an ancient cedar-tree (the cedar is sacred throughout India), the families of the village taking it in turn to provide the victim; the tree was cut down many years ago. *

See Frazer, J. G., The Golden Bough (Abridged edn.) ch. ix

The case of the singing woman, of course, was of a nature almost bound to come to light, but there is many an alleged virgin sacrificed in the dry riverbeds in India at dead of night when the annual flooding fails to take place; and such is the religious nature of this immolation that the whole of the caste will naturally form a conspiracy of complete silence on the matter. Practices such as this, of course, are allied to that of the human offering to the rain-god, and another in the same category is the frequent kidnapping and sacrifice of a boy to appease the god of a new water-tank, the body being buried in the foundations.

Mr. Sarat Chandra Mitra, an Indian anthropologist, in a paper to the Anthropological Society of Bombay, which I heard in 1934, expressed the opinion that an ascetic of Aligarh, in the United Provinces, a strong centre of Kali-worship, actually sacrificed to that goddess his *chela* (disciple), of whose murder he was found guilty, being sentenced to death. This ascetic had built a shrine to Kali, with an underground cell below it in which he lived with his disciple, who vanished. He was convicted on the evidence of a bloodstained knife in his possession, and on the disproving of his story that he had been attacked by two robbers. He told the court that the goddess appeared to him in a vision, demanding sacrifice, but he thought it meant the offering of cockerel or animal, and carried this out; he could not explain the disappearance of the disciple.

To the scientific inquirer, there is at least the moral justification of honest motive for the good of the community behind the human sacrifices carried out in the agricultural ritual, but there can be no such justification for the most terrible of all human immolation in India, that of a Devadasi, or temple dancing-girl and official prostitute, who is slain if she fails to please the god at her initiation.

There are very few temples now at which the once-famous Devadasis are maintained officially and openly as part of the temple establishment, but two of them are, strangely enough, in the heart of the jungles of Goa, that part of India which has been officially Christian for the longest time: In the Goan hinterland are these two very ancient temples, those of Kamaksha, with a wealth of fourteenth-century sculpture, and Shiroda; they are the only ones the buccaneering Portuguese spared when they Christianized the country at the point of the sword under that ruffian admiral of the sixteenth century, Affonso de Albuquerque, and the fanatical "Saint" Francisco Xavier. Here are gathered amazing ancient Hindu treasures, some of which I was privileged to see, thanks to a custodian who did not object to western archaeologists (especially one who took the trouble to appease the deity with several rupees).

The temples are close together, and to the establishment are attached Devadasis, with their own houses; the girls I saw were of breathtaking beauty as to face and figure, and they extended seductive invitations; but one resisted, bearing in mind that eighty per cent of the Indian population have some form of venereal disease.

In exploring the jungle region around the temples, but tactfully out of sight of them, in daylight, a European companion and myself accidentally stumbled upon a shrine of Siva, which consisted of a built-up stone platform some three feet high and three feet square, surmounted by a lingam, the conical stone erection which is the symbol of Siva and represents the human penis. This lingam was about three times the size of the human organ, and as it bore fairly fresh bloodstains, and we had heard rumours regarding sacrifices, our suspicions were aroused. Through the mysterious way in which whispers circulate in India we learned a little later that this was the spot chosen for the initiation of Devadasis, and that an initiation-rite was due to take place at the full moon, a few nights thence.

We said nothing, but on the appointed night, having first witnessed quite openly one of the oldest dances in the world, a mere foot-shuffling movement around a huge kind of maypole in one of the temple courtyards— a crop-fertility ritual dance—ewe crept away to a place of safe concealment in the jungle from which we could witness the Devadasi ceremony.

What happened is not to be forgotten to one's dying day. The rite proceeded in a normal way, with mantras and a mock-marriage to Lord Siva, who is the apotheosis of all the sex-symbolism in Hinduism, and who was represented by a sword. Then came a trial by ordeal, to discover if each girl candidate in turn was acceptable to be the bride of the god. This was performed by stripping the girl naked after the mock marriage, and, after one of the priests had sucked her nipples to arouse passion (presumably for the god), forcing her down upon the stone lingam until its whole length, over a foot, was inserted in her body, so that she sat on the platform.

One girl alone made a sound; she let out an agonizing scream, which is not surprising, since the Devadasis are supposed to be virgins at their initiation, and her agony on the breaking of the membrane and distension of her organs by this huge lingam can be imagined. She was instantly removed, and the priest slit her throat with a knife, offering the body to Lord Siva at the foot of the platform with loud apologies, while another officiant placed the next shuddering girl on the phallic symbol, down which her predecessor's vaginal blood was still running.

It was not until later that I learnt by very guarded inquiries that any girl who utters a sound during the ordeal is deemed thereby to be rejected by the god as unfit to be his bride, and must be sacrificed; any Hindu will vigorously deny the whole ceremony. Needless to say, my friend and I did not go to the police; had we done anything so foolish, our lives would not have been worth an anna. Moreover, we had both lived in India long enough to know the unwisdom of encouraging interference by the "secular arm" in a Hindu ritual, however unfortunate its consequences in this case; and I must admit we took the view that the girl was better dead thus than exposed to almost certain death from syphilis as a priestly prostitute, anyway.

The form of purely voluntary human sacrifice called sati, a widow's self--immolation on her husband's funeral pyre, is an act of renunciation that cannot be regarded as *felo-de-se*, as all suicide is by the Anglo-Saxon alien rulers of India who try to suppress it. The basis of Hindu thought and belief is that one can never cease to exist; the body is burnt to ashes, but somewhere beyond, there is a conscious existence in which one may enjoy the company of the loved one just as in this life. Nothing is more natural', says the Hindu, than that his wife should wish to enjoy his company in this future state. Moreover, the practice is by no means so terrible as English officials try to make out, for the Brahmin priests have knowledge of certain herbs, whose juice, rubbed into the woman's skin with sandal-paste, makes her insensible to fire. My friend Levante, the great western illusionist, was able while touring in India to prove that this or a similar juice was used on the soles of many of the firewalkers, who show no traces of burns after walking across a bed of red-hot coals.

The practice of *sati* will die hard; not only is it fully supported by Indian orthodoxy, but in some castes, such as the Tottiyan and Uppara, the household gods are actually representations of female relations who committed sati, and as recently as June 1932, a widely signed subscription list was circulated at Masulipatam, seeking funds to raise a monument to the memory of a Hindu girl-wife who had committed the act in the previous May, and the scene of whose sacrifice was a daily resort of large numbers of pilgrims.*

Miles, op. cit., 39.

The most bizarre practice in all the world connected with the notion of human sacrifice is to be found in India. It is based on the weird belief that a leper never dies completely, and even the most educated of Indians affirm this. Consequently, as a last resort in case of a prolonged drought, when all other magic has failed, the agricultural population of south India dig up the body of a leper (since these unfortunates are not cremated), and either burn the corpse or throw it to the jackals or into the river. The men of the hilltribes explain this by avowing that this ceremony "almost equals human sacrifice", and declare that, unlike other corpses, those of lepers are found undecayed if dug up a month after burial.* The people clearly believe they are sacrificing an ever-living being. Incidentally, an Indian leper is always buried with a quantity of salt, with an eye to the future use of his cadaver for the rain-magic, it being thought that the rite will otherwise be ineffective. Salt probably acts somewhat as a preservative, but I should think the real reason for its use lies in the universal belief that evil spirits fear salt, and that they will not, therefore, devour the corpse; in either case the motive is to have a nice, juicy leper-carcass handy and more or less undamaged in case of need.

Ibid., 256.

Finally on the subject of human sacrifice, there frequently occur in India cases of what might be termed ecstatic suicide. I recall in particular three instances, which show the lengths to which the Hindu's beliefs will carry him. One, which reads like a page from the Middle Ages, comes from the town of Chanda, near Nagpur, where stands the ancient temple of Mahakali, a form of the primitive earth-mother goddess. Here a worshipper named Rameshwar, who was in financial difficulties, prayed to the goddess for relief; but his prayers were unanswered, and his moneylender continued to dun him. Enraged, Rameshwar dashed into the temple and hurled a stone at the image of the goddess, just grazing its face. Later, he was overcome by remorse, and took his life.

The second case provided a Bombay Hindu hotel with a first class sensation and wide, if undesirable, publicity. A Hindu lawyer staying there dreamed that his favourite god, Balareshwar, called on him to leave this mortal plane and join him in heaven. This the lawyer did by swallowing opium, after leaving a note for his friends explaining his action.

The third example came from Papanasam, south India. A young Brahmin of the Vaishnavite sect (the worshippers of Vishnu) made a fire near a neighbouring village, where he was leading a life of meditation and devotion to his family god, Sri Ramachandra, and jumped into the flames, calling "Rama, Rama!" He died despite the efforts of a passing Muslim to rescue him. The suicide left a letter stating that he took his life deliberately, in order to reach heaven.*

*Times of India, 16 May, 1934; 20 June, 1933; and 12 July 1933

Hindu fanaticism, in addition to the actual taking of life, leads its devotees to perform the most amazing self-tortures, chiefly in south India, and mainly in connection with the worship of Kali in her various forms. Even readers almost totally unversed in Indian matters will have heard of those extraordinary *sadhus* who pass their days sitting on a bed of spikes, or with long pins stuck through their flesh; but these performances are nothing, and the men assure one that through long practice of yoga and intense concentration they feel no pain and suffer no harm.

To such a pitch did self-mutilation by devotees of Kali in the southern Mariamman rites attain at its celebration in May 1933, however, that in consequence of a fanatic fatally injuring himself the Coimbatore police chief interfered, with one of those peremptory emergency orders beloved of the British official in India, forbidding the practices of self-mortification, and putting a posse of police on guard. I have information that the order was apparently obeyed openly, but disregarded in secret at dead of night—as such orders always will be. The police cannot forbid a Christian nun to wear a hair-shirt if she wants to; why, then, should they have power to poke in their infidel noses if a few fanatics choose to torture themselves, or even by their sacrifice to reduce the overpopulation of 350,000,000 in India, eighty per cent of whom have syphilis, anyhow?

The chief self-tortures indulged in at this Mariamman festival of Tirupur were the dragging of the great *jagganaut*, the car of the god, by ascetics pulling it with ropes attached to hooks piercing the muscles of their backs. They even brought the practice up to date; one devotee was thus seen dragging along a heavy motorbus loaded with worshippers, and another a lorry, to attain merit with the goddess. In view of what we have said of the Khonds and their beliefs, it is of interest to note that this Mariamman festival, which is undoubtedly an attenuated substitute for human sacrifice, is held to be definitely of Dravidian (and therefore pre-Hindu) origin; and the worshippers are principally non-Brahmins, of Dravidian stock. Hence, in the present writer's view, those who hold that the Brahmins are responsible for the continuance of these and other rites of self-torture are mistaken, for the roots of the practice lie in far more ancient and primitive magico-religious practices than the Hindu superstructure.

An individual act of worship involving self-torture, which is still practised in regions remote from the authority of a magistrate, is that known as Chidi-Mari, in which a temple attendant beats the devotee's ' back-muscles into insensibility, and then hoists him, by ordinary butcher's hooks stuck through his back, some ten feet into the air. This is entirely voluntary, and is usually undertaken as a kind of penance, as, for instance, when a man believes that his poor crops are due to the displeasure of the gods, and that nothing will overcome it but the intervention of Mari-amma (Kali) who must be persuaded by this sacrifice to act on his behalf. Nearly always the devotee works himself into such a state of ecstasy that he professes to feel no pain after the ordeal, and he will often walk as much as twenty miles home immediately afterwards. Owing to police interference, the sacrifice is becoming modified in the more populous district, a little wooden figure being substituted for the human body and subjected to the hook-swinging.

Sights to which the European can never quite get accustomed without feeling sick are witnessed in south India during the full moon period of February, in connection with another torture sacrifice known as Taipusan, a form of pilgrimage under torture. The devotee will walk miles to a shrine on spiked sandals, the spikes sticking into his feet, with many pounds of lemons pinned or hooked into the muscles of his body; sometimes, too, he carries on his shoulders a spiked board on which is mounted a heavy erection of teakwood. Other fanatics cover every available inch of their bodies with pierced tridents of Siva, only leaving their legs free for walking, and balancing on the tridents a heavy brass vase full of sacred *ghi* with which to anoint Siva's lingam, symbol of the penis. Not satisfied with this, they brand large patches of their legs with red-hot irons before starting out, to increase the torture.

Another common spectacle is that of a man with skewers piercing his cheeks from side to side, undertaken as a vow of silence to paralyse the tongue, and endured for days, during which time the devotee is fed only with liquid poured into the mouth. After these instances it can well be imagined what sufferings are inflicted upon "lower orders" than man, the unfortunate animals whose sacrifice has always been coincident with, and is now largely substituted for, human offerings in Indian temple rites.

Chapter 5

Animal Sacrifice

As we have hinted in the preceding chapter, animal sacrifice in the majority of cases is a substitute for the human offering, a fact well demonstrated in the mime-magic performed by the Malayali caste of Salem district to fool a demon when it demands a human sacrifice. Weird designs are drawn on the ground with yellow paste, and a man, much camouflaged with paint, leaves, and rags, dances among these patterns. His left arm is cut with a knife, and when the blood spurts out he covers his face with it by waving the arm about. A chicken is then decapitated, and the performer sucks its blood from the neck.* We have already noticed a somewhat similar case of substitution in the Lambadi's plague fleeing ceremony.

*Miles op. cit., p. 30.

Another clear demonstration of origins is seen in a widespread south Indian custom, since the banning of *meriah*, of shaving a sheep or goat, draping a man's *dhoti* garment round its body, putting a hat on its head and a caste-mark on its forehead, and then sacrificing it as a human being. Again, the Khonds today use buffaloes, goats, and sheep in their sacrifices to the earth-goddess, admittedly as substitutes for the *meriah*.

As is to be anticipated from its origin, the chief and most ancient purpose of animal sacrifice in India is to ensure the fertility and health of the crops and cattle, or to bring down the rain. The later stages of belief, in their probable order of succession, are to purify a family after death—this being connected with ancestor worship; to appease tree and other spirits for taking their dwelling, as when bamboo is cut; for divination in illness and other matters; and to placate the deities of disease in an epidemic.

It should here be remarked that there seems to be no significance in the use of a particular animal; where one caste or tribe will kill a buffalo, another may use a pig, sheep, goat, or chicken indifferently, it being the fact of blood that matters in every case. One looks in vain for such definite evidences of totemism in this respect as are found elsewhere in primitive cultures, and one can only conclude that Hinduism has absorbed aboriginal totemism into its pantheon. This will be clear from a very simple instance: the monkey is nowhere sacrificed in India except in the very low culture Nayadi caste, who offer its flesh to their own three godlings and prescribe it as the food of a pregnant woman in her sixth month; it is everywhere sacred, not by virtue of being the totem of any particular caste or tribe, which it is not, but because it is the symbol of the god Hanuman.* I can only find in all Indian customs one definite instance of a tabu in the subject under examination: in ancient days the Malayali of Salem used, like the Greeks, to sacrifice horses annually to the sun, but now worship the horse; and the Masulipatam weaver caste of Kurubas do not ride the horse because it is the vehicle of their gods.**

*There can, on the other hand, be little doubt that Hanuman only became a god after being a human leader of a tribe using the monkey totem; his part in the great Mahabharata epic points clearly to this origin, and the same applies to the Nagas, or cobra-clan, discussed in Chapter vii.

** Even The present immunity of the horse from sacrifice can hardly be totemistic, as we have the evidence of the Ramayana epic for the royal performance of horse-sacrifice in the earliest days of Hinduism.

Taking the rough classification of animal sacrifice above in the order given, we find several examples that well illustrate its agricultural significance. The Khonds have a buffalo-sacrifice in this connection. Having first danced in drunken frenzy round the beast until it is stupefied, they smother it with caresses, and then sing over it a dirge entreating it not to blame them for what they are about to do, after which the animal is taken to a sacred grove and tied to a stake. Here the men throw off to their women all possible clothing and again enact the frenzied dance, at the end of which the one acting as priest hits the buffalo on the head with an axe, and the dancers hack at it with their knives. Each man, as soon as he secures a lump of flesh, rushes off to bury it in his fields.*

*Miles, op. cit., p. 84.

There is a filthy and primitive tribe in south India, the Kuruvikkaran, who, when it is time for their festival to Kali, piles seeds into five heaps; if, on being counted, their number does not agree with a forecast by the diviner, the festival is put off for a year. When it does take place, nine goats and buffaloes are sacrificed, and a member of the caste, after sucking the blood from the throat of a goat, is able to answer oracular questions regarding such matters as crops (though these people are now mostly nomads).

A rite performed ostensibly to ensure the health of the cattle for the ensuing year, but which seems to have originated in the crop fertilizing ritual, is seen at festivals in the Godaveri district, where a pig is buried up to its neck in the earth, and cattle are driven over it until it is trampled to death.*

*Miles, op. cit., p. 30.

Undoubtedly agricultural ritual lies behind at least the climax of a long seven day festival held yearly by the Nayars of Calicut in honour of Bhagavati, whom we have already noticed as a form of the earth-mother, and who, in Indian legend, slew the giant demon Asura.*

*The illiterate in Malabar also regard her as responsible for smallpox, and propitiate her with goats and fowls.

At this climax, on the final night, after a devil-dance by two lads got up to represent the boy-satan Kuttichchattan and his friend the demon Gulikan, four goats, one given by each of the owners of the temple, are decapitated by the priest, who wears red silk robes. Several cocks are next slaughtered, and the priest sprinkles charcoal powder and saffron over their bodies. The carcass of one goat is then dragged out of the temple by the priest's assistants, who are blindfolded and taken three times round the building, to the chanting of mantras. After this the assistants uncover their eyes and cook some of the goat's flesh with rice. This mixture, with much saffron powder (the use of which is probably, as I explained earlier, to serve as a "giver of life"), is then buried in the ground. Finally, the priest simulates demoniac possession, running wildly round the temple scattering rice and yelling mantras, and all that remains is to remove the corpses and clean up the mess for normal worship on the morrow.*

*Miles, op. cit., p. 259.

In another cock-sacrifice ceremony, in Cochin State, the worshippers, both men and women, publicly make water and evacuate on the idol before slaying the birds, with the utmost indecency, yet solemnly, as an act of devotion. I can only conclude that this ritual pollution of the shrine, never allowed at any other time, is a survival of sympathetic magic based on the idea of producing fertility by imitative manuring.

An illuminating seed-planting ceremonial survives among the Cheramans of Malabar They assemble for it in front of a barn door that has been painted with rice-water. A lighted lamp is placed on the floor near the door, and cups are made out of leaves for as many varieties of seeds as there are in the barn. The owner of the barn, accompanied by a man who carries the cups in a new basket, opens the door, and the others follow them in and fill the cups with seeds, calling on the gods and ancestors of the caste.

All then proceed to the fields, where part of the ground has been decorated with flowers and leaves. A new ploughshare is fastened to a new plough-frame, and a pair of bullocks is harnessed to the latter. Both bullocks and plough are painted with rice-water, and the man carrying the cup-basket makes a mound of earth on which he sprinkles cow-dung and throws a handful of seeds. The bullocks are then driven in one wide turn with the plough, the furrow forming a circle, inside which some smaller furrows are ploughed.

The plough-handle is next dropped, and *puja* done to Ganesh, the elephant headed god. A coconut is broken on the ploughshare, and from this divination is done. If one piece be much larger than the others the harvest will be moderate: if the eye of the nut has been broken through, it bodes misfortune. Into the piece of coconut holding the most milk, a leaf of the *tulsi* plant (a symbol of fertility throughout India) is dropped. If the leaf turns to the right there will be an abundant harvest, but if to the left, calamity is foretold. At the end of the seeding ceremony a goat is sacrificed to Muni, the protector of bullocks and farmers, and its blood sprinkled on the ground.*

Miles, op. cit., p. 264-5 91

We next come to sacrificial ceremonies of which the basis is ritual purification; their origin is ancestor-worship and the ghost propitiation that is its natural corollary. This being one of the earliest forms of religious belief, it is not surprising to find these rites only among the very lowest groups, least touched by Hinduism, such as the Nayadis, Khonds, and Todas.

The Nayadis are indeed the lowest of all; they eat lizards, rats, and crocodiles, and "Pollute" Brahmins at a greater distance than any other community. Their own three godlings, Mallan, Malavazhi, and Parakutti, are very obscure, and they chiefly worship ancestors, whose souls are represented by mere piles of stones. During worship these stones are sprinkled with the blood of a sacrificed chicken, and the ancestors are asked to drink it and to protect the tribe from wild animals and snakebite.*

*Ibid., p. 128 - Ibid., p. 87

The funeral ceremonies of the Dravidian Khonds are very interesting, and differ from those of any other caste; they will be discussed in detail in a later chapter, but a point which interests us here is that a death requires a purification ceremony by the family, for which purpose a buffalo is killed on the seventh day after death, except when a man was killed while hunting, in which case a pig is sacrificed. The head of the animal is cut off and passed between the legs of the men assembled for the occasion, and if it touches anyone's legs it is a very bad omen. This ritual is similar to that of certain Nigerian tribes which drive the ghost through a cleft bamboo to get rid of it, and the Khond idea appears to be that the ghost departs thus in the head of the slain animal, since a loud noise is then made to frighten away the spirit. The Khonds also make doubly sure by providing a scapegoat in the shape of a sheep, which is tied to the feet of the corpse and trots along with the bearers to the burning-ground, where it is left until five days later, when it is sacrificed with corybantics similar to those we have described as occurring round the *meriah*-post.

Among the Todas, that aboriginal tribe of the Nilgiri hills whose origin is a matter of great interest and perplexity to anthropologists, a buffalo is usually sacrificed to conclude a funeral ceremony. A bell is tied to its neck, and its horns are smeared with butter before it is finally despatched by blows from a club. This is generally done before the cremation, though sometimes afterwards; in the former case the deceased is laid out on the animal's back, with his feet on its horns and his head on the rump. Very often the Todas disinter the skull from the spot where the cremated bones have been buried which is a good instance of ancestor-worship in embryo, but I have never heard of their preserving a series of family or headmen's skulls, as do many African tribes.

A more advanced group, the Kuruba caste of weavers, who bury their dead and take precautions to prevent the spirit from troubling its relatives, kill sheep and chickens after the funeral and give the whole village a feast, but it is not clear whether this has much to do with either purification or spirit-appeasement.

LOST WORLDS AND UNDERGROUND MYSTERIES OF THE FAR EAST

One Indian caste, and I believe only one, sacrifices an animal as scapegoat for the purpose of purification when a woman is discovered "misconducting" herself. So low are sexual morals throughout India that no notice is usually taken of such a matter. However, in this caste, the Kapu, the members of the household concerned, sit round, and a black goat is carried thrice in a circle, then decapitated, and its head buried; and on that spot the guilty couple must tread, while water mixed with turmeric, which has been previously offered to the god Ganesh, is poured out. Usually the "shame" is purely format and is made the excuse for the inevitable feast, "a happy time being had by all", as the reporters would put it.

Along with the conception of wandering ancestor-ghosts needing propitiation goes a belief in equally exacting tree-dwelling spirits (often inaccurately called animism); of the two, it is impossible to say which, if either, is the later development. In the Guntur and Bellary districts is found the tribe called Bonthuks, who are mainly nomadic, though they do cultivate to some extent. Their chief occupation is collecting bamboo, straightening it by fire, and selling it in the bazaars. Before collecting it they always sacrifice, ostensibly to the local god, but obviously to propitiate the spirit dwelling in the bamboo, a sheep, a goat, and a few chickens; the god is merely represented by a heap of stones.*

*Miles, op. cit., p. 162. 3

The Kallans of Madura, whose bargain with any strange god on a thieving expedition I described earlier, have a very ill-defined religion. Ordinarily classed as Saivite, they are really devil worshippers. They believe that certain trees are occupied by demons, to which they make offerings of rice and milk under such trees, with a little fire lit so that the demon can see the oblation. If such a tree grows in the jungle, and is thus off the beaten path, a sheep or goat is sacrificed and its blood spilt at the roots. The devil, the Kallan says, will then come out of the tree and enter the body of the worshipper, who thus becomes the devil's mouthpiece and can act as an oracle on events of the immediate future; and on the devil returning to its tree, the man comes out of his trance.*

*Miles op. cit., pp. 139, 140

This belief differs from the usual idea that the spirit enters the body of a slain animal, probably because there is here no question of a scapegoat or a magical act to drive the spirit away. The beliefs of the Kallans need more investigation; they make animal sacrifices to rather vague river-deities, but none to their own caste-god Alagarswami, because he is held to be a vegetarian!

We may here conveniently consider a few miscellaneous cases of animal immolation which fall into no definite class. The most naive of these is undoubtedly that practised by the sect of mendicants known as the Donga-Dasari ("servants of the god").* Their chief deity is the monkey-god Hanuman; they are professional burglars, and before setting out on a thieving expedition they ascertain by divination if it is his pleasure; this they do by placing a turban on the head of a sheep and then sacrificing it by decapitation. If the turban falls off on the right side the expedition may safely proceed, but if on the left it is an ill omen, and the gang returns home to await more favourable auspices.

*Ibid., p. 12 6

Divination of another kind is employed in association with animal-sacrifice by the Badagas and other south Indian castes whose gods are mainly agricultural. They throw water over the animals selected for sacrifice, and accept only those which shiver when it falls on them. Whether this is connected with ideas of ensuring rainfall by homeopathic magic, or whether it is associated with the widespread primitive notion of a "water-barrier" against evil spirits, I have not been able to ascertain. The Badagas worship the lingam and have elaborate milk tabus, but have no other water rites.

A definite water-rite, practised chiefly among the maritime states of the Kathiawar peninsula in north India, is the sacrifice of a goat at the launching of a new lighter or a fishing-boat, the sea mother goddess being invoked under the name of Mata. Our European custom of breaking a bottle of champagne at the launching and naming of a new ship is a relic of such practices, common throughout the seaboard of pre-Christian Europe, and derived from the Viking sacrifice of a horse to Thunor before crossing the seas on a raid. Rather remarkably, since they are an inland people, members of Nepal missions to Europe always do puja to the sea god at Bombay harbour before leaving, and on their return.

So influenced has Muhammedanism in India been by Hinduism, that when in January 1934 Dureshwar, a daughter-in-law of the Nizam of Hyderabad, the greatest Muslim ruler in India, returned from a voyage to Europe, four goats were placed before her on disembarking at Bombay, and she performed over them a magical rite called *sadka,* to ward off the evil eye.* These animals were not killed, but Islam does indulge universally in a goat-sacrifice at its great annual festival of Baqr-Id.

Evening News of India, 8 Jan. 1934.

Sacrifices to fire, though it has its own god, Agni, are not common in India. One recorded by Miles * as witnessed in a southern jungle involved the following ceremony: a sheep was rubbed with oil and painted with vermilion stripes; its horns were garlanded with flowers, and its ears, nostrils, and mouth stuffed with dried grass. After several men had dealt it heavy blows with sticks and stones, one choked it to death by pressing his knee into its throat. The worshippers then cut open its stomach and pulled out the entrails and all the fat they could tear loose. They held the fat over a fire of brushwood, letting it liquefy and fall into the flames; finally they hacked the carcass to pieces, some frying huge lumps in *ghi* before eating it, and others devouring it raw, letting the blood trickle down their faces. No god was invoked, nor was an image of one visible.

Op. cit., p. 29

This, there seems no doubt, was a fire-purification rite; but occasionally we hear of a case in which a sacrifice is performed as a malicious act of defilement. One such case, which had a touch of humour, resulted in a number of men being charged in court at Sinnar with criminal intimidation and "disturbing an assembly engaged in religious worship". Arising out of a family squabble, the defendants, hearing that the complainant was preparing for worship of the family god, sacrificed a goat on the doorstep and tied its corpse before the door, just as everything in the house was ready for the ceremony, with the result that the whole place was effectively polluted, and the priest could not enter.*

Times of India, 5 Jan., 1935

Throughout India a vast number of castes and tribes propitiate their tutelary deities with animal sacrifice simply to keep in their favour; a few examples will suffice. The Pongalas, a division of the Reddis or Kapus, who number more than 2,000,000 and are the largest caste in the Madras region, do this at their central temple, Perambalur, by drinking goats' blood before the idol of their goddess.

Those members of the Valmikudu hunter-community who annually propitiate their village goddess by giving a buffalo for sacrifice are exempted from paying house-rent. These people have an interesting tabu: the priest must not be seen, for fear of misfortune to the village, while he is engaged in the sacrifice, or when he subsequently delivers a chunk of the carcass, with some of the blood, at each house in the village.* The Valmikudu also propitiate a number of minor deities with goats and sheep.

*Miles, op. cit., p. 99

Kali is worshipped with animal sacrifices by the Devangas of Madura district under the name of a tribal goddess, Chaudeswari. The whole community attends here; there are elaborate pollution tabus, and after the slaughter the rest of the ritual is chiefly a sword balancing feat by the priest to divine whether the temple has been polluted or not. The Brahmin priest, for all his hauteur, is not above accepting a nice fat sacrifice even from a polluting caste, such as the Paidis of Ganjam, who have to pass in their offering of a goat or sheep to the temple, and must watch the rite from beyond polluting distance of its doors. Being "unclean", they can only share the benefits vicariously, which they do by taking home a pinch of the earth outside the temple and placing it on a clean cloth, with offerings, before their village god Takurani.*

*Ibid., p. 262

The most quaint reason for any animal-offering in India is that of the *dhobi*, or washerman, when during January he propitiates his caste-god Madivalaya, in whose honour he makes models of his boiling-pots and the slabs on which clothes are beaten, with offerings of eatables. He sacrifices a sheep or goat, and sprinkles the blood over these images; he stoutly avows that this is not done to propitiate the god, but to ensure that the clothes will not be burnt or spoilt in the boiling-pot. It seems rather a farce, for no Indian *dhobi* will ever boil clothes properly, and the ceremony makes no difference to his absolute genius for ruining one's shirts and sheets by bashing holes in them on the jagged rocks of the seashore. You are compelled to impose a scale of fines for damage, and one month these were so heavy that they completely cancelled the wash-bill, a fact which my *dhobi* accepted with philosophical resignation!

It is now time to examine the last class of animal sacrifices—those connected with disease—whether of cattle or of the human community. An amusing incident occurred when I was staying in so-called Christian Goa, which illustrates how thinly the veneer overlies the latent paganism of the Goanese. My host kept missing some of his finest white cockerels, for several days in succession; he had his suspicions, so finally, on the night of the full moon, we kept watch, hidden in the deep shadow of the steep verandah steps to this fine old Portuguese manor-house. In due course a dim cloaked form emerged at the side of the house leading to the servants' quarters, making frantic efforts, as it slunk across the compound, to stifle a clucking noise emanating from under the cloak.

It proved, as we had suspected, to be my host's native butler, making off with another choice cock. Seized, and frightened into a confession, this worthy admitted that he took the birds to the village witch-doctor for sacrifice and divination on his wife's illness. This was a Sunday night; that same morning the butler, got up "regardless" in an amazing medley of bits of European costume, his Sunday best, and dutifully attended Mass at Curtorim church as a good Catholic. Even the village priest in Goa rarely knows who the witch-doctor is, and even when he does he shares the villagers' tenor of that individual too deeply to betray him, for most of these priests themselves are Goanese sons of the soil, half educated and as superstitious as the Hindus they are supposed to convert. We could extract from the butler no details whatever as to the form the divination took.

Although he maintained a grim silence, however, one can conjecture the probable method from the practice of the Paidis of Ganiam, who consult a sorcerer if anyone of the caste is seriously ill. The magician goes to the patient's house and draws on the floor, with rice, a square divided into several compartments, in each of which he puts copper pice, while a dish of cooked rice is put on one side of the square. A fowl is then sacrificed, and its blood poured round the dish. The sorcerer then throws rice into the dish, a grain at a time, uttering the name of a god or goddess at each grain. If a grain sinks, the deity whose name was mentioned when that grain was thrown in has caused the illness, and must be propitiated as the sorcerer directs.*

Miles, op. cit., p. 262. -9s.

To preserve their villages from both cholera and cattle disease the Chembrambakam caste of south Indian Lingayats propitiate their god Namamdamma with a blood-sacrifice. A goat is killed and its intestines placed in a pot, which is covered with a piece of the goat's skin. A low-caste man must then carry the pot to the village boundary and bury it there. It is

76

believed that anyone passing the man while he is so engaged will fall seriously ill and probably die; once the pot is buried at the boundary the goddess gives her promise that no cholera or cattle-plague will break out in the community. Here we have two features of interest: first the significance of the intestines, which should be compared with that in the *meriah* rite, and probably has the same origin; and second, a tabu similar to that against seeing the Valmikudu priest operate. The hater feature seems to involve an idea that, should the man with the pot be met, the potential evil imprisoned therein might escape and transfer itself, whence it is necessary to bind it firmly by burial outside the boundary.

When an epidemic of any kind has actually broken out among the Madiga, a leather-working caste of the Telugu country, they sacrifice a buffalo to their god. Its head is cut off, and the blood is poured over boiled rice. The head, with one of the legs stuck in its mouth, is then placed before the shrine in one basket, and the rice and blood beside it in another. A devotee next puts the animal's head on his own, with a lighted lamp on top of it. He twists round his waist a rag which has been dipped in the blood; ropes are tied to his body and held by men who follow him; and limes are cut into pieces and thrown into the air all round him to prevent the evil spirits, who watch from behind all the trees along the road, from following him. The man then passes in front of the houses whose owners have subscribed to the ceremony. This festival was actually witnessed during a plague epidemic in a southern village by Miles, who states* that he was told that sometimes, instead of the bloody rag being worn round the waist, the animal's intestines were pulled out and the devotee draped round his middle with them, the ends trailing in a gruesome fringe.

*Op. cit., pp. 29, 30

There has of late years been an increasing tendency among the more enlightened Hindus themselves to agitate for the abolition of the mass-sacrifice of animals which takes place during cholera and smallpox epidemics, and of which the chief centres are Nasik in the west, Kali Ghat at Calcutta in the east, and the Ellore temple in the south. Thus, late in 1933, the Hindu reformer, Sir Purshotamdas Thakurdas, succeeded in persuading the priests to abandon the centuries-old animal-slayings in the temple of the goddess Singotari at the seaboard town of Hajira in Gujerat; here, following a signed agreement on the matter, a procession was made to the *kund*, or sacrificial slab, and it was solemnly destroyed by the *pujaris* (temple priests) themselves.*

*Times of India, 2 Jan., 1934

It was a small beginning, certainly, but it was the only kind of approach that will effect any change. English methods, such as the favourite magisterial ban, and proposed legislation in provincial Assemblies, do nothing but "set up the backs" of the orthodox, and substitute, for open slaughter, the secret jungle rites of torture. This statement is not made in prejudice-indeed, the present writer has no concern with politics, and is wholly free from prejudice on the ethics of animal-sacrifice one way or the other, his sole business being the cold, scientific examination of customs; but is made in the light of what has happened time and again when such prohibitions have been imposed.

Speaking of prejudice, this is usually so violent on the part of western observers that it is but fair to give a statement of the Brahmin's case for animal-sacrifice. This, in a sentence, is the belief that, having been sacrificed on a holy occasion, the animals have attained salvation, and will not again be born as animals. Further, he holds that the very stability of the universe depends on sacrifice, as the gods feed upon the spiritual part of the offerings. We have no more evidence as to the truth or the falsity of these views than we have for the accuracy or otherwise of a Christian's view of heaven; both are entirely based on human speculation and man-made concepts of the gods and of the hereafter.

Scientific training and common sense, however, cause one to condemn the religio-magical proceedings attendant upon the terrible outbreak of cholera at Nasik in May 1934, solely because these rites resulted in a great spread of the disease through the huge concourse of pilgrims they attracted, thereby completely neutralizing the efforts of the medical corps to fight the outbreak; on the other hand, it may conceivably be argued that India is so overpopulated by its 360,000,000 undernourished and mostly weak-minded inhabitants that the elimination of a few thousand by natural plague is not an unmixed evil. However, we are not concerned with the ethics of the matter.

The records, as culled from the Nasik newspaper correspondents' reports throughout the May, make amazing reading. The proceedings began in the middle of the month with the sacrifice of a goat at the Bhadrakali temple, to propitiate Manai (a form of Kali), goddess of destruction, in order to free the town from the cholera scourge. No one, of course, thought of giving this filthy place a general scavenging as a start. From early morning a great stream of pilgrims, finally estimated at more than 10,000, poured steadily to the temple to make offerings before a huge sacrificial fire. Chanting mantras, the priests installed outside the temple a Mang (low-caste) woman, after giving her a ceremonial bath and arraying her in a new dress and green bangles, green being a life-giver symbol. She sat, her face veiled, receiving from the women pilgrims' offerings of coloured powders and coconuts, also magical "givers of life"- copper coins, and cloth.

Late in the afternoon the priests poured scalding-hot rice into a specially prepared cart drawn by decorated bullocks, the rice being then covered with the red powders known as *gulal* and *kunku*, much used in Indian magic, while incense from the side of the sacrificial fire was set ablaze in the cart.

A comic anachronism was that the procession which then formed up was headed by the Nasik Boy Scouts' band, playing European music. Next came a man bearing on his shoulders the black sacrificial goat; a second man, leading another goat, for dedication to the goddess; and a third carrying a cockerel. The Mang woman followed, accompanied by priests, and there was also another woman, who, allegedly "possessed" by the goddess, danced furiously through the ranks of the procession nearly naked, and with dishevelled hair. Then came the cart, on which, as it passed, those standing along the line of route down to the river threw rice, as also they did on the Mang woman.

A stampede occurred, in which a number of people got hurt trying to seize a pinch of the "blessed" rice from the cart; and the next thing that happened was regarded as an evil omen: the axle broke, before the shrine containing the idol of Manai was reached.

About four miles out of the town the priests had baskets full of rice carried round the head of an image of the goblin Bali, and performed a number of ancient magical ceremonies. After this the Patel of Nasik (a cross between a headman, mayor, and chief constable) chopped off an ear of the sacrificial goat before it was killed and handed it over to the Mang woman, the other goat being simply dedicated to Manai and set free.

Eight selected persons next carried eight baskets of rice from the cart, spells having been chanted over them, and threw down the contents at the eight cardinal points of the town, to prevent the evil spirit of cholera from re-entering it. All the remaining rice was dumped and left in the middle of the main Trunk Road.

The whole procession, except the Mang woman, who was left behind (as a ceremonial scapegoat or medium for transfer of the evil) and had to return to the town on the morrow, then went back to Nasik, where the Brahmins took a much needed ceremonial bath. The whole of this performance was a revival, after many years in abeyance, of a very old magical ritual, and the wily priests who organized it, and who of course did not care two pins whether the disease abated or not, made a small fortune out of the pilgrims' offerings.

As was to be expected, far from the rites stopping the epidemic, the huge concourse of people caused it to spread even more, and it is a fitting commentary on the competence of Indian guardians of the law that the Nasik gathering was allowed despite a ban by the district magistrate on gatherings of more than twenty-five people during the outbreak. One of the fresh fatal cases proved to be that of a man who had taken rice from the cart; and the local medical officers had not even the courage, or the will, to put the whole town in quarantine.

Worse, however, was to come. A week later the epidemic was raging more seriously than ever, and had spread to surrounding villages, whose half-starved inhabitants had obtained the infection through making a feast of the rice dumped on the Trunk Road, after it had been contaminated by the loathsome pariahs, or pi-dogs, which are efficient cholera-carriers. The waters of the very sacred, and consequently very filthy, River Godaveri, on whose banks the temples of Nasik stand, were also infected, and carried death far and wide in the district. The priests' explanation of their failure, of course, was that Manai had not been sufficiently appeased.

At the same time as the Nasik devastation the coastal town of Ratnagiri also had a cholera visitation, and here events were not without a touch of humour for those of us who can view these matters with scientific detachment. When the outbreak occurred, the local temple priests saw a golden opportunity, and seized it. They discovered that for the previous three years the customary annual sacrifice of twelve goats to the alleged town-deity, Sri Bahiri, performed as a bribe to him to keep the town free of epidemics, had fallen into abeyance, and they declared that the arrears had angered the god, who had consequently sent the cholera and must at once be appeased by the sacrifice of the thirty-six goats due to him.

The Khots, the local temple trustees, gave a naive explanation for the lapse: it seems that years ago the Government made an annual grant of 66 rupees for this sacrifice, of which the Khots got only 34 rupees, 14 annas for the purchase-price of twelve goats; meantime goats had gone up in price during the previous three years; hence the sacrifice had been dropped. The Khots did not explain what had happened to the money during those years, but they thought it best to be on the safe side of the god, and managed to raise sufficient to buy forty-eight goats—the thirty-six due as arrears and the twelve for the current year; these were duly sacrificed, and the installment account with Sri Bahiri was brought up to date.

There was a more happy ending here than at Nasik, for the epidemic rapidly abated thereafter, and, much to the annoyance of the Nasik priests, those of Ratnagiri crowed over them, claiming the success of a superior magic, and attributing the decline in the cholera to the full appeasement of Sri Bahiri-carefully omitting, of course, to give any credit to the health measures taken by their own more enlightened municipality.

It is in south India that the most wholesale slaughter of animals, and the most reprehensible torture of them, is found. The proceedings at Ellore, also in May 1934, aroused a storm of protest. It was the first time for seven years that so great a mass-slaying had been held, and in one day 500 animals and 500 fowls were immolated to appease the goddess of smallpox, Poleramma, who is again Kali in another form; her shrine and worship had been installed in the town during the previous five months, owing to an outbreak of the disease. Numerous petitions to magistrates, and even to the High Court of Madras, by animal-welfare societies seeking to get the slaughter prevented, were completely rejected, and the animals came along in great numbers, given by families afflicted with the disease, or wishing by an offering to avoid its visitation. Eight persons were appointed to decapitate the animals and fowls, working in relays.

All day the holocaust went on, and the climax was reached at midnight, when eight selected male buffaloes were slain. The chief priest, wearing robes soaked in the slaughtered animals' blood, then led a procession through the town, bearing aloft, on a tray full of rice and blood, the head of the biggest buffalo, and chanting hymns to the goddess, while a mixture of rice and blood was strewn along the route. The next morning, huge figures of the goddess, painted on placards called *prabha*, and a cart in which sat the priest, still in his blood-drenched robes, were taken out in procession though the streets; and this was the end of the rites, the priests announcing that Poleramma was now fully appeased, and that the scourge would leave the town—which, of course, it did not.

At the same time arrangements were made for holding other similar sacrificial festivals at different points in the town during the next fortnight. Before the first of these was due to take place, more futile petitions presented by animal-lovers were cold-shouldered by the local magistracy on the ground that "no breach of the peace was feared". The rites duly took place, 700 animals and 1000 fowls being butchered in one street alone, and at the end of the final ceremonies rice mixed with their, blood was strewn all round the confines of the town so that the smallpox demon would not enter the area thus magically protected.

Immediately afterwards there was a concerted move against such practices, led by the Bombay Humanitarian League and the Madras S.P.C.A.; but as both bodies were largely under European inspiration, no practical result accrued. It is of interest to read the statements of the ex-president of the Madras body, Mr. Justice Jackson, on the subject of the tortures to which, in that part of the country, sacrificial animals are often subjected:

"The limbs and ears of sheep are torn from their bodies piecemeal before they are actually done to death" (I record above the severing of the live goat's ear at Nasik).

"In sheep-sacrifices, sometimes the animal is cut up while alive into 32 pieces, and its flesh taken bit by bit. This is done at dead of night, to avoid an outburst of public opinion against it.

"Even pregnant sheep are offered for sacrifice, the young being pulled out by hand from their wombs and killed first, and the suffering mother despatched later.

"Live pigs are thrown from a height on to sharp spikes planted in the ground, and left impaled there in agony till the pile on each spike reaches a certain height. They are then removed for others to take their place.

"Buffaloes are imprisoned in pits specially dug for the purpose, then pierced with sharp swords in several places by a number of persons standing around them; and after the infliction of much agony the head is finally severed.

"Fowls offered in temples are tossed up and down by time-honoured custom, and are also bitten and their blood sucked while alive.*

Quoted in Times of India, 27 June, 1934

This document is a serious indictment of one of the worst phases of Hinduism; even if the civil authorities at Ellore were wise, as they probably were, in refusing to stop the sacrifices there and thus risk a serious riot—for they knew that in the Ellore rite no torture was involved, it being held an ill omen if the animal were not killed with a single axe-blow—steps should certainly be taken by the Hindus themselves to put a stop to the tortures revealed elsewhere in Madras. They form no part whatever of the higher teachings and ideals of Hinduism, in which there is much that is fine and worth the attention of the West; the faith has suffered, as do all organized religions—Christianity, perhaps, most of all—from indefensible accretions.

Chapter 6

The Magic of Images

WIDELY divergent as are the magico-religious practices obtaining throughout the world, there is one idea so widespread that we may call it common to all regions: the belief that a vague, mysterious magical power lies latent in all things, a power supernatural and immaterial, for which the most familiar name is that given to it in the Pacific, *mana*. This belief, shared by races right across the world, from Polynesian to American Indian, has been called "the mother-idea of magic", and it has become to some extent confused with animism, which strictly should only be applied to a belief in a sentient spirit inhabiting plants and stones.

While it is impossible to give in detail here the thesis of culture diffusion, which ascribes the origin of these conceptions to the early agricultural ritual of Egypt, a very brief outline of it, and of Egyptian funerary ritual, is necessary for the understanding of many Indian customs and beliefs, for it seems certain that the Egyptian conception of the indwelling power of the statue as the abode of the *ka*, or spirit of the deceased, bound up with the practice of mummification and the theory of the divine saviour-king has left its mark throughout the world. Curious and direct survivals of it, indeed, are to be found to this day, not only in the Far East, but also, in a distorted form, in southern Europe, whence a belief in the protective efficacy of wax images spread at an early date from Egypt through Greece.

The aim of mummification was to secure immortality, which the Egyptian regarded not as being purely spiritual, as does the Christian, but in terms of complete body and spirit; he believed that anyone who had been embalmed with the correct magical rites, and for whom the subsequent necessary tomb-ritual had been performed, was assured of eternal life in the land of the dead ruled over by Osiris, by virtue of the fact that, by mummification itself, the deceased was identified with Osiris, the first king who died. As time went on, of course, the theological accretions to the original idea led to a complicated belief in a judgment of the dead and his "trial" by the Forty Gods in the underworld; but we are here only concerned with the matter in its primary details. Probably the most striking survival of the belief in corporeal resurrection entire, in the modern world, is the uncompromising Muslim tenet that those who have been decapitated cannot attain paradise.

Consult the works of Elliot Smith and W.H. Perry.

The coming into being of the practice of mummification, and of ideas of continued survival of the dead in another place (called in early texts Sekhet-Aaru, which may be translated as Fields of Bliss), caused the king of Egypt to be regarded as an incarnate Horus, son of Osiris. The living king was charged with the maintenance of the cults attaching to his dead father, who was thus identified with Osiris, and provided him with food necessary for him to remain alive in the other world, materialistically conceived as a glorified replica of life on earth. Also, the king performed the ritual necessary to reanimate the body of his dead father, or his portrait statue as substitute for the mummy, in order that the dead king might partake of the food and hold communication with the living.

The cult has thus a dual aspect; it may be regarded as the cult of a god-king, or as ancestor-worship. As Elliot Smith puts it: "Osiris was the prototype of all gods ; his ritual was the basis of all religious ceremonial; his priests who conducted the animating ceremonies were the pioneers of a long series of ministers who, for more than fifty centuries, in spite of the endless variety of their ritual and the character of their temples, have continued to perform ceremonies that have undergone remarkably little change."*

*Evolution of the Dragon, p. 32.

The Egyptians themselves, indeed, claimed that all funerary cults originated with Osiris, that he gave them their doctrines, religious rites, rules for the sanctuaries, and plans for the temples. With later changes, such as the predominance of a solar cult due to political causes, we are not concerned ; Osiris himself crops up, as we spread eastwards from the Mediterranean, in an amazing and unexpected variety of forms. We find him featuring later as the Babylonian culture-hero Oannes, and still later in a similar guise as Prithu Wainya, the Shining One of the Indian Puranic myths, whose description of him is identical with that of Oannes, and there can be little doubt that the cult reached India through the Sind "gateway" of Mohenjo-Daro. This is discussed more fully in our next chapter.

Having been embalmed, the Egyptian body was on the day of burial subject to elaborate ceremonies re-enacting incidents in the resurrection of Osiris. It was especially necessary, by powerful charms, to open the mouth and ears of the deceased, that he might speak and hear in Sekhet-Aaru ; and the ritual-magical literature of this procedure finally swelled into the collected rites known as the **Book of Opening the Mouth**, though its chief ceremonies had been practised as early as the late-Neolithic and pre-dynastic epochs.* The mummy, in its coffin, was then lowered down the tomb-shaft and placed in a stone sarcophagus, and food, drink, toilet articles, a magic wand, and a number of amulets for protection against enemies of the dead were left with it; the shaft was then filled up with rubble.

Budge, E. A. W., Book of Opening the Mouth (London, 1909), vol. i, p. viii.

Outside the burial-chamber was a small chapel-chamber, beside which was a tiny ante-room. In this latter there was walled up a portrait-statue of the deceased, with small channels cut to connect the room with the offering-chapel, so that the ka, or double, of the man might attach itself to this statue and, though those channels, enjoy the food and drink placed in the chapel. In early times the "opening of the mouth" rites were performed actually on the body; later they were transferred to the ka-statue. It is outside our purpose to go into the metaphysical distinctions which the Egyptian made in those parts of human personality surviving after death ; suffice it to say that at the crucial stage of the mouth-opening magic, the Kherheb, a chief priest of a class which throughout Egyptian history is associated with magical power, declared that the ba, or heart-soul, and the ka, or double, had taken up their abode in the statue.

Finally the funeral feast took place, and its details show us plainly the origin of the Christian "sacrament" of Mass. The spirit part of the offerings was consumed by the gods, the ka and the ba, and the material part of them, eaten by the officiating priests and the relatives of the deceased, brought these human participants into communion with the beings of the other-world, and thus with Osiris. A theological development in thought led ultimately to figures of workmen, known as ushabtiu, or "the answerers", being placed in the tombs of the great, after being endowed with magic, to ensure that the dead man's spirit would have the spirits of his labourers to work for him in paradise.

We are now in a position to understand some of the Indian beliefs on the subject of images and their power. It is by no means uncommon to find miracles attributed to them, and of this the most extraordinary case on record is one, well authenticated, from Travancore State, communicated to me by Mr. Padmanabha Iyer, a journalist of repute in the State and a Hindu of considerable education. In the Changanur temple of that State there is a metal image of the local goddess which, incredible as it seems, actually menstruates once every four or six weeks, and the temple records show that this phenomenon has been observed regularly for at least a century.* The Travancore government even makes special provision for expenditure in connection with the Trippuvarattu, or purification ceremony, attendant on the occurrence.

See Travancore State Manual, ii, 89-90

The loin-cloth round the image is sent to the women of the Vanjpuzha or Taiavur Potti caste for examination; they pronounce the discolouration to be menstrual blood, whereupon the image is removed to a separate shed (as is the case with a woman under this pollution in many Indian and African tribes) and the inner shrine of the temple is closed for the duration of the periodicity, the goddess being taken back to it on the fourth day. The discoloured cloth is sought after by the people as a holy relic.

It is recorded that when an Englishman who held the office of Dewan (a kind of Prime Minister in an Indian State) paid his visit to fix the expenditure budget of this temple, he refused to sanction the amount allocated under the heading of the purification ceremony; but the very next day the image obligingly commenced its menses, and the Dewan had the cloth shown to an English-woman, who vouched that it bore genuine menstrual blood; and to this day the expenses on the ritual bear the seal and sanction of the European official!

It has never been suggested that the phenomenon is a fraud performed by priests putting round the image a menstrual-cloth from a female devotee; but, of course, it would be impossible for an English official to obtain such test conditions at the shrine as would be necessary to investigate the matter, owing to the rigid caste and shrine-defilement tabus. No non-Brahmin would ever be allowed by the priests to keep a watch in the inner sanctuary.

However, there may be some connection between this queer affair and the magical ideas of blood as a life-giver which are involved in a legend that the progenitor of two south Indian castes, the Reddi Bhumalu and the Pokunativaru, was born from one of the sanitary-pads thrown off by Parvati, the consort of Lord Siva, with whom she is represented as living in his heavenly Kailasa in a state of constant sexual connection.

Whatever be the truth in the case of the menstruating image, Travancore can produce another equally inexplicable. In the Thirunakara temple at Kottayam in that State there is a famous image of the Nandi, or bull of Siva, made of granite covered with bronze, which on five recorded occasions, at long intervals, has allegedly oozed blood through a small opening in the left side near the tail. The latest recorded instance of this miracle* was on the morning of 17 July, 1934, and it appears to be well vouched for by eye-witnesses, while the blood was certainly real, and was sent to the Maharaja at his capital, Trivandrum, in a *puja* vessel, while special services were thereupon conducted in the temple. Whether the priests have some wily trick of inserting the blood overnight into a secret cavity it is impossible to determine; but local legend says the bull was once alive, and wandered by night destroying crops, whereupon it was hunted down and wounded in the side, so it staggered to the temple, lay down before the shrine, and was found next morning there turned into stone.

Times of India, 19 July, 1934

It is a peculiar fact that to quite a number of Saivite nandis is attached the legend that they were once alive, and that there are attributed to the king-bulls of sacred herds in India many miracles which it seems impossible, owing to their details, to collate with the cult of the cow; she falls into another class, connected with the worship of the earth-mother. The chief group of king-bull miracle legends is found among the Karumpuraththals, a caste of Kanarese speaking farmers chiefly inhabiting the Madura and Tinnevelly districts — again in the same region as Trivandrum.

Examples are: During a fight between two castes at Dindigal the king-bull left on the rock the permanent imprint of his hoof; which is alleged still to be visible; during a later quarrel between the same castes another king-bull stopped the sun and made it turn back in its course, resulting in quick arbitration owing to the shadow which thus fell from a tamarind-tree. The Karumpuraththals never milk their cows, and bury their bulls with honour, regarding the king bull as the living Nandagopala, after the god Krishna the cattlegrazer.

There was a strange manifestation of animal-worship, which led to the creation of a fresh nandi image and shrine, at Sheikhapura, in the Punjab, in 1934. A sacred bull died in one of the filthy, winding streets of the bazaar, and instead of being left, as is usual, for the Untouchables to remove, was actually lifted on to a cart by the caste Hindus, who usually will not touch a carcass, and taken with full funeral honours to a spot where later a mausoleum was erected over it, with a bull-image into which the spirit of the dead bull was believed to take up its abode.

There is considerable room for "miracle-working" fraud in connection with the images of the goddess of smallpox, Mariamma, because, although an ancient Hindu injunction forbids the making of idols in wood, probably owing to the white ant's ravages, hers are usually made of a kind of red wood which when punctured oozes a red sap which in appearance is very much like blood.

One up-to-date case of the Indian belief in an indwelling *mana* attached to images, though rather vitiated by facts savouring of sectarian propaganda, does at least illustrate the conception. This was a strange report appearing in the papers* from Bangalore in July 1934 that the skankam and chakram, the symbolic devices of Vishnu, the preserver-god in the Hindu trinity, held in the hands of the idol now known as Sri Venkateswara (a form of Vishnu), had begun to shake, making it necessary to secure them to the idol with strings, though there were no earthquake tremors to account for their sudden instability.

Times of India, 29 July, 1934

The devotees said this image was formerly a Subramaniya idol of the other great sect, the Saivites, or worshippers of Siva (the destroyer-god of the trinity), and was subsequently converted into one of Vishnu. They also alleged that the symbols in the hands were not there when the original shrine was set up, and hence they declared that the idol was protesting, by trying to shake off the symbols, against its "forcible conversion" to the uses of the Vaishnavite sect!

Closer within my own personal experience comes a weird adventure, and a phenomenon open to no such suspicions of fraud as those just related, which befell a friend who is a Brahmin, an erudite scholar, and a deep student of the ancient Tantric magic of India, Mr. Vishnu Karandikar, of Poona. While we were engaged in certain archaeological investigations at the temple of Old Mahableshwar in 1934 we discovered a very rare object; a small image of the ancient goddess Gayatri, with four faces. The priest flatly declared that we would not be able to get a photograph of it; he said I should not, in any case, not being a Brahmin—unless certain magical rites were performed first, since the mantra of Gayatri is the most powerful known to Tantric students. Partly because he wanted to see what would happen, and partly because, having lived long in London, he has an extremely skeptical outlook, Mr. Karandikar went to turn the image, which is only some three feet high, in order to get it into a more favourable light for his picture. Though easy to handle, as regards bulk and size, it absolutely refused to move, even by our joint efforts, and when Mr. Karandikar tried again, alone, he received from some invisible force a violent blow across the left hand, which raised a weal and broke a thick gold ring he was wearing.

In addition to this, when he still persisted in his efforts to get a photograph of the image without performing *puja*, every plate of the subject came out clearly as a picture of the wall against which the image stood, but with no idol visible on it, though camera and plates were all in perfect order, and the rest of the batch of plates had already given perfect pictures of other objects and buildings round the temple. My own luck, with an equally good camera and plates, was no better; so finally my Brahmin friend did perform the ancient magical incantations prescribed by the temple priest, and was able to photograph the image, and a very evil thing it is to look upon. I too made another attempt, after the ceremonies, but could get nothing but a blurred outline of the idol, though the wall behind was sharp. Another queer experience on this expedition was that Mr. Karandikar was also unable, until *puja* had been performed and offerings made, to get a picture of the entrance to the lair of the sacred cobra on Mahableshwar Hill, at which snakehole the priests daily make offerings of eggs.

It is very widely believed in India, as elsewhere, that to photograph an image robs it of part of its power (that is, its *mana*) and causes some portion of its personality to leave the image. Agricultural castes such as the Badagas go so far as to maintain that the whole virtue of their gods would depart if they were photographed, and that they would be unable thereafter to do their work of looking after the crops; it is more than one's life is worth to attempt to get a picture of these huge, grotesque deities.

Experiences such as those I had at Mahableshwar are things that cannot be explained by western science, and when one has the evidence of one's own eyes, combined with a scientific training and a habit of mind not easily fooled by the tricks of priestcraft, it were foolish to deny that there does exist a great deal of occult influence in the ancient holy places of India. One experience of this, which is absolutely first-hand evidence, concerns my own researches at an ancient site near Bombay, and is related in its appropriate place in my concluding chapter.

A curious and interesting example of the belief in the indwelling god in a statue comes from Kottakal, Malabar, communicated to me by a fellow-member of the Mythic Society of India from Calicut in January 1935. In that month the inhabitants of Kottakal, in consequence of a serious drought, sought to obtain the blessing of Siva for rain by a ceremony in which the chief rite consisted of pouring 1001 pots of water daily over the head of Siva's image in the local temple, "to cool the god's head", as they said—an instructive case of sympathetic magic, it being thought that the god was parched like the land, and that his slaking would slake the land. The number 1001 has no special, significance; in India all contributions are made in an odd number, a round figure being held unlucky.

This ceremony, according to the devotees, was based on experience, for, on the occasion of a parallel drought thirty years before, it was performed, and the rain fell in torrents on the seventh day from the start of the god-ducking. This time, however, though they doused the deity for the full twelve days prescribed, no rain fell, and local theology was at a loss to explain it. The case is instructive as showing how coincidence (for possibly on the previous occasion the rainfall was nothing more) often bolsters up a belief; also, the rite is a good example of homeopathic rain-magic.

An even more illuminating instance of this, also involving an image, is the rain dance of the Rajbansis, a nomadic tribe who originally emigrated from Sikkim and are now found all over the Terai district. Somerville* describes the rain-dance as he witnessed it, remarking that it is performed by women only, it being regarded as very unlucky for a man to see the performance.

*Somerville, op. cit., 194 sqq.

This dance was done by the Rajbansis of Cooch Behar, the original inhabitants of the district, in a small jungle clearing beside the half-dried bed of a stream. About twenty women, mostly young girls, but including some old hags, appeared, bearing in their midst drums and cymbals and the image of a deity called Hudum Dev, a god of great repute in the district. The image was of mud, and painted red—a significant point, being associated with blood as the life-giver. The women set the image in the centre of the space and proceeded to watch the moon, until it was practically fully risen overhead.

The old women then started the musk, a rhythmic drum-beat punctuated by cymbal-clashes at intervals. The minute the music began the young girls sprang up, stripped stark naked, formed a circle round the idol, and began to dance, uttering a wild, plaintive chant. At first their movements were slow and graceful, and they "seemed to be pleading with the god for the special favour of rain", but as the dance went on the music became louder and more compelling, the movements of the dancers swifter and wilder, and their chant fiercer. Working themselves up into a fury of contortion, they no longer pleaded with the god, but hurled curses upon him, spitting at the idol. Both song and dance then became very obscene, and in a final burst of fury the girls fell upon the idol, smashed it, and scattered the bits in all directions. This done, the music ceased, and the girls put on their clothes.

This vituperation of the god when he fails to do his duty is a common feature of ceremonies which attempt his compulsion by magic; and the breaking and scattering of the idol is obviously a relic of the early agricultural sacrifice of a human victim to bring rain or crop-fertility, in which the head and blood of the victim were thrown on the fields. Should there be any signs of rain during the Rajbansi dance, the ceremony ceases and the god is reinstated with full honours in a triumphal procession. Whether the tabu against men witnessing the dance is originally bound up with the association between the blood-symbol, female menstruation, and fertility magic, or whether it is due to the necessity of protecting the girls against the habitual lasciviousness of the Indian male, one cannot say, but Somerville notes with amusement that despite the ban there was quite a crowd of men, from youngsters to old rakes of about ninety, ensconced in the pipal-trees, feasting their eyes on the naked dancers.

A minor example of a rain-rite in which homceopathic magic is combined with the *mana* of an image is that of the Reddi or Kapu caste of Madras, which here again is performed by women. Making a clay figure of a child, they place it on a cloth, hammock-fashion, and walk with it from door to door, singing indecent songs and begging alms. Each householder from whom they beg pours a little water on the image, and this is supposed to produce rain.* An Anglo-Indian acquaintance tells me that when he last saw this ritual, the women took it in turns, as they reached the houses, for each to lift her skirt, exposing herself (Indian women wear no drawers), and to make water down her legs as she stood: highly indecent, no doubt, but very interesting as a piece of sympathetic magic.

*Miles, op. cit., 266 4

A widespread device in India to ensure pregnancy is only comprehensible on the basis of the *mana* belief. This is, for women to eat the powdered scrapings of sacred boulders or of old statues of gods*; and analogous to it is the belief that if an infertile wife spends the night in a shrine, sleeping at the foot of the idol, the god will impregnate her. One would not like to count the number of proud Hindu "fathers" who, rendered impotent by inheriting generations of early marriage and the results of their forebears' venereal disease, have some wily Brahmin priest to thank for the gift of a son!

*Sarat Chandra Mitra, in paper to Bombay Anthropol. Soc., Dec. 1932

The belief of the women, however, is a natural one, deriving as it does from the early Mediterranean-culture conception of the personality dwelling in the statue; this has also an echo in the universal Indian belief that the gods eat the food-offerings placed before their images, and another in the uniform custom of bathing the idols in the -sacred rivers and tanks at certain festivals, apparently with the idea of ceremonially purifying the dwelling place of the god.

Thus at Nasik the image of Maruti receives this ceremonial bath once every twelve years, and in Travancore the Maharaja bathes that of the family's tutelary deity twice yearly in the sea at a special festival called Araat.

The *mana* of an image does not diminish with the passing of the years; only pollution (with the exception of such ceremonial pollution as we noted in the previous chapter) or utter decrepitude causes a temple idol to be replaced. The belief in its continued efficacy as the abode of the deity is well illustrated by an extraordinary incident of which I heard when in Lahore in January 1935. In a Punjab village called Jandiala Sher-khan, not far from Sheikhapura, a Brahmin named Chulab Bass, being short of money, sold an aged pipal-tree to the local blacksmith, a friendly Muslim. The latter, cuffing it down to use the timber on repairs to his house, found inside the trunk a small image of the goddess Durga (Kali; no doubt it had been placed between two small trunks, which had coalesced in the course of centuries. That same day the Brahmin's wife fell seriously ill, and the blacksmith's son was stricken with high fever; the Brahmin repented of selling the tree, fearing he must thereby have committed sacrilege against the goddess.

The most striking evidence as to the widespread survival of the early Egyptian beliefs on the significance of the statue (and, concomitantly, on mummification), however, is to be found in death ceremonies. India can furnish us with a few examples, among which is the practice of the Khonds, whose funerary rites, as we have already noted, differ from those of any other caste, and whose indigenous tenets as a whole seem less overlaid by Hinduism than those of others. The day after a Khond cremation, a dish of cooked rice is placed on the spot where it occurred, and the spirit of the deceased is requested, with incantations, to eat and enjoy itself. The spirit is specially invoked not to enter the body of a demon or tiger, in which forms it could return and annoy the village. Three days after death, an effigy of the deceased is made in straw, and set up on the roof of the hut he inhabited. The friends and relations then assemble and lament before the effigy, each bringing a present, and receiving one of greater value from the family on departure.*

*Miles, op. cit., 86-87.

Then follows the buffalo sacrifice I described in the last chapter.

The Odde, a caste of Kanara potters, who bury their dead, make an effigy of the deceased out of mud after the interment, and offer it cooked rice and fruits.*

*Ibid., 147

The Bonthuk nomads, who also inter their dead, place food in the deceased's hut for the spirit to eat; when he is presumed to have had his fill, it is put in a basket, in a hut specially built for the occasion near a stream, to feed the spirit servants of the god of death: a very clear survival of the Egyptian rite in the *ka*-chamber!*

*Ibid., 163.

To understand these rites and their significance more fully we must turn to parallel practices elsewhere, notably in Nigeria, where C. K. Meek, whose work is a model of careful anthropological research, has discovered very strong evidence of Egyptian survivals.** One of the most striking of these cases is found in the burial customs of the Cabin, a tribe of the Adamawa province, who expose on a table for three or four days the bodies of all old men and women, giving the relatives time to assemble and do honour to the dead before interment. When the body swells up and bursts, the skin and intestines are removed and buried separately in a pot. We have noted the Indian treatment of sacrificial intestines, and also the fact that the human organs were placed in ancient Egypt under the protection of certain guardians of the dead. The Kilba and Verre tribes follow the same practice with the skin and intestines as the Cabin.

**All Nigerian details from Meek, C. K., *Tribal Studies in Northern Nigeria*, ii, pp. 312, 377, 400, 439 sqq., 463, 511, 514. 540, 559, 592,608*

While the corpse is exposed, all the people gather round and throw over it the seeds of the various crops, with the expressed intention of conferring upon the deceased everything he had in life: here we see a relic of the custom of making the dead person an Osiris. After burial, a mock corpse is made, consisting of a pot round which a gown is draped, if the person was important, and round it the people dance for two days. Here we have obviously a distorted vestige of the Egyptian *ka*-statue, and Meek rightly holds that the removal of the skin and viscera are degraded forms of the practice of mummification, also derived from Egypt.

An even clearer case of the *ka*-statue survival is found m the ancient rites of the Hona tribe, also of Adamawa province, which are still observed (with the exception that the chief's death is no longer kept secret for a month). When the death is announced, a representation of the chief is made, consisting of a log of wood covered over by a white gown. This is held by an official seated on a basket, and all bow down before it and cast over it the seeds of corn, beniseed, and pumpkins, saying: "See, we give thee corn, so that thou shalt not say we have sent thee away hungry." A dance is then performed, during which the effigy is fanned, and after this the corn thrown over the effigy is collected and made into beer and flour for use at the subsequent funeral.

Meantime the effigy is dismantled, but its place is taken by a pot with a strip of cloth round the neck, which pot is set up on a forked branch beside the dead chief's hut and carefully tended by his widows till the funeral feast, at the end of which it is smashed, to signify that the chief and his people have parted for ever. From this procedure one gathers that the idea is to keep the chief dwelling with the tribe, first in the log, then in the pot (these objects serving as *ka*-statues), until his obsequies are completed. The straw effigy of the Indian Khonds has just the same significance.

A custom of peculiar interest and importance, illustrating as it does several points at the same time—the statue-rite, the Osiris, and the king as living vehicle of the life of the crops—is that practised by the Yungur-speaking people of Pirra, N. Nigeria. When a priest-chief dies, no public ceremony is held till the following March, i.e. till the planting season is close at hand. Then the chief-elect makes an effigy of his predecessor, which is not a crude log or pot, but a likeness, having head, ears, eyes, nose, body, and legs. The head is covered with a cap, the body with a gown, the feet with sandals; the effigy is then set up in a public place, and all do honour to it with great awe, each person throwing guinea-corn over it.

At the end of the day a maternal relative of the dead chief comes and takes the effigy away, depositing it in a cave in the hills, and it is said that immediately on his return the first rains begin to fall. The Yungur, Meek states, hold the idea that as the chief had been performing the annual rites for obtaining corn during the month of March prior to his death, the crops for that year belong to him, and thus, if he dies before they are harvested, they too would die and go with him. The fiction must therefore be maintained that he is still present with his people, and he must continue to be present until his successor has carried out the rites for the following year, in the next March.

Precisely the same idea is found among the Jukun,* for when a chief dies his death is kept secret, and the crops harvested that year are held to be his. The Jukun are additionally interesting, because they are known to preserve the bodies of their chiefs by a process of fumigation, and in March they remove such a "mummy", and deposit it in some secret place. Though Meek suggests that what is allegedly the chief's preserved body may really be only an effigy, he recognizes that even the practice of making an effigy is connected with mummification and the *ka*, wherever it be found; and that of desiccating the corpse by fumigation is even more so, while it also forms a survival of the practice of censing the *ka*-statue.

The Jukun customs are described by Meek in another work, A Sudanese Kingdom, but are alluded to passim in the book cited.

The Yungur-speaking peoples seem to regard all old men and women as "owners of corn" in a minor way, for they make an effigy of them, as well as of a chief, at death. This attitude may be explained by the function of woman as the repository of life, and of the aged as the repositories of the life of the tribe. Possibly some obscure reasoning of the same kind would explain why among the Hindus very old persons and infants are buried, not cremated.

Returning to the question of throwing corn on these effigies, two explanations are given by the people themselves. Some say that the object is to provide the dead man with seed to plant new crops on his return to this world; others, that the seed was given him to plant in the next world. The latter is probably the truer explanation, and it has its parallel, and apparently origin, in the Egyptian custom of placing the germinating figure of Osiris in the tomb. Still further evidence that with the Yungur-speaking group every old person is an Osiris is to be seen in the custom, among their southern section, of dropping the body of an aged person on the ground every hundred yards or so on the way to the grave, the idea being that, as he is an "owner of corn", this bumping will make him leave the corn behind.

I once came across a very curious parallel to this in England, in a former custom that bodies being taken from the hamlet of Glen Parva, Leicestershire, to the parish church of Ayleston, had to be scraped and bumped (in the coffin, of course) across a certain stile on the footpath. No-one knew why, but the reason vaguely alleged was that it was "something to do with preserving the right of way", which, of count, was nonsense, seeing that the right of way was already established by the parish's immemorial usage of the path. Returning to Nigeria, we may compare the Yungur custom with that of the Jukun, whereby the dead chief is besought not to take the corn with him, in answer to which an official, to whom the dead chief is strapped on horseback, knocks out of the corpse's hand a quantity of grain.

Meek has a most illuminating chapter (ch. xv) on the subject of the divine-king cult in Nigeria, from which we have only space to cull a mere outline germane to our present thesis. Speaking of the Jibu, he points out how strikingly their burial rites show traces of the Egyptian "opening of the mouth", the object among the Jibu being to give the dead man sustenance, in the shape of the sacred beer, that he may become an Aku, or living spirit, a member of the ancestor-group. After further rites, steps are taken (as was done in Egypt) to wipe out the footprints of the Aku, and a chicken is sacrificed, its blood being offered to the spirit, as we have seen in Indian ceremonies. In India, by the way, many castes at their death ceremonies take the precaution of preventing the spirit from haunting the living by means of the "water-barrier", the sprinkling of water and the breaking of its container. Some of the Cameroons tribes pour libations of the sacred beer over the skull of a dead chief, which in this instance seems to serve the same purpose as the *ka*-statue.

The chiefs of the Kam and Jukun are closely associated with corn, and carry out a daily ritual by which they feed the royal ancestors, particularly the last deceased king, who is regarded as the life and soul of the crops; thus they play the part of Horus, living son of Osiris, as did the Pharaohs; the Nama of the Cameroons go further, holding that upon the goodwill of the royal ancestors depends the success of agricultural operations, and among them, the fact that the living chief is the incarnation of the life-giving power of the crops leads to his apotheosis after death. Ancestor-worship, which is equally prevalent among many Indian castes and tribes, is thus seen not as an undeveloped, primitive form of belief, as it is so often represented to be, but as a disintegrated survival from the complex theology connecting kingship with agricultural fertility.

Finally in connection with the cult arises the interesting problem, to which we have already made allusion, as to whether (as Frazer firmly holds) the old king was actually killed in the early Mediterranean culture. I have suggested that in some of the Indian *meriah* and animal-sacrifice rites we appear to have a substitute for the killed king; and even more suggestive is the fact that among the Kanakura, a Nigerian tribe of Adamawa province, the chief of the Shani area until recent times "fled" ceremonially to Buma after a reign of ten years, and by exchange the chief of Kombo, fled to Shani-apparently to keep alive the vitality magically vested in the chiefs.

It is in Melanesia, however, that the early Egyptian beliefs on the significance of the statue, which have only left in India such traces as we have examined, survive in their most typical form; and this region is the chief stronghold of the belief in *mana*, which is the dominant feature of the religio-magical culture. It is here associated with certain spirits called *vui*, who appear to be the traditional representatives of the sacred chiefs of the archaic Mediterranean culture; these *vui* have much *mana*, and are closely associated with stones.*

See Perry, Origin of Magic and Religion, p. 168, and Codringtons: standard work, The Melanesians.

There are certain features of Hindu mythology which very strongly suggest a distorted survival of this in India, much overlaid by the innumerable complications of the pantheon and the "incarnations" of the gods. One of the simplest examples is the legend of the god Vishnu turning himself into a *salagrama* stone, which is a fossil ammonite. The story is that a low-caste dancing girl, whose head was turned by her own beauty, could find no mate to match her, so retired to the Himalayas to fast and meditate. Here she met the god Vishnu, whose beauty excited in her an uncontrollable sexual passion, but, owing to her low status and her profession, he pretended to remain cold to her advances (another version says he had to be discreet on account of the jealousy of his consort). In the end Vishnu compromised by promising that the girl should be reincarnated in the form of a river, and that he would lie in its bed, in the form of a *salagrama* stone, as her eternal lover. Thus was founded the Gandaki River, and the incarnation of Vishnu as a "precious" stone. The description in the ancient Skanda Purana of this lying-together is a prize piece of pornographic literature, as are all Hindu stories of the gods' amours.

The consequence of the legend has been that great wealth has come to Nepal, whose ruler farms out the concession of getting the ammonites from the river-bed. Though it has no intrinsic value, the stone is held in such high reverence that the Vedas decree that a Brahmin's house without a *salagrama* is as impure as a cemetery, and any food cooked in it as unclean as a dog's excrement. To touch water in which this stone has been washed is to receive absolution from all sin, however heinous, and to drink such water assures a place in the ultimate heaven.

There can be no doubt, not only from this, but from many other indications in his legends, that the shining Vishnu, like Prithu Wainya and many other type-heroes, represents a form of the *vui*, and of the divine ancestor-cult from the archaic culture. Incidentally, it is highly interesting that this same fossil ammonite is the very stone into which our "Saint" Brigit of Ireland is alleged to have turned the serpent; the origin is identical." Indeed, the whole of the world's mascots are ultimately traceable to the power of *mana*, and the magic of the image.

The halo of magic and legend that thus grows up around the statues of the archaic culture and their derivatives cannot be better illustrated than by two stories yet current: one in southwest India concerning the megalithic monuments, found only in association with early gold-mines (notably in the

Nizam's dominions), and the other on Easter Island. The Indian legend is that the great monoliths and dolmens, which, of course, represent the burial-places of the wandering gold-seekers of the archaic culture from the Mediterranean, were somewhat vaguely "put there by the gods". The story told by the people of Easter Island regarding their immense, mysterious mono-lithic images amounts to the same thing, but is more picturesque, and is given in a preliminary report, published in the **Christian Science Monitor** during December 1934, on the work of a Franco-Belgian educational expedition engaged in collecting all the folklore of Easter Island, and its remains.

"Once upon a time," say the natives, "a god carved the great statues, and as soon as they were finished he bade them walk; and all of them arose, and took up their stations on the great rock altars built to receive them, the chief among them remaining on the slope of the volcano-crater to form the court of the sculptor-god."

That portion of Melanesia in which the belief in *mana* is most highly developed—the northern New Hebrides and the Banks Islands—is full of the remains of the archaic civilization; and there is even a connecting link with Egypt among the people of Ponape in the Carolines, where the early people practised the art of making portrait-statues, through which alone the gods can be approached, by ceremonies which were performable only by the sacred king of Ponape.

We have now to consider another aspect of the magic of images which, though parallel to that outlined, is applied not for the worship of the honoured divine ancestor or the assistance of a dead person's spirit, but for the purposes of sorcery.

Even before mankind attained settled habitation in the Mediterranean region we find in the food-producing stage of culture (or, as Sollas terms it, the Age of the Ancient Hunters) attempts made in this direction, and this early sorcery may well claim our attention for a moment, since an example of it has recently been discovered in India which in detail is indistinguishable from its European prototype.

In the late palmolithic and early Neolithic caves of southwestern Europe we find a certain feature which leaves no doubt whatever that prehistoric art was magical and thereby utilitarian: in its origin, and not executed for art's sake.* This is the series of cave-paintings of animals shown with arrows and spears piercing their vital parts, which depictions were unquestionably, by sympathetic magic, to ensure the success of the hunter. To mention merely a few cases, the caves of Niaux, Portal, Tuc d'Audoubert, Trois-Fréres, Montespan, and Cabrerets have fine examples. A practically contemporary instance, coming millenia after these cave-paintings, and corroborating this view as to their use, is the behaviour even now of pygmy hunters in Central Africa. Professor Frobenius in his reminiscences describes how his pygmy huntsman went through a magical rite of drawing an antelope in the sand and spearing it, to ensure good hunting before setting out, and how on the return he propitiated the antelope-spirits with some of the hair and blood of a slain animal.

Count Bégouen, "The Magic Origin of Prehistoric Art", in Antiquity, vol. iii (1929).

Again, Count Bégouen, to whom we owe much in the study of early-European magic and art, holds that certain so-called "tectiform" signs in the cave-paintings do not, as is generally supposed, represent huts, but animal-traps; and they strongly resemble traps in Helsingfors Museum, made by the Lapps to snare wild beasts.*

Op. cit., P. 10.

Now, it is very extraordinary that a series of rock-paintings has been found in recent years up on the Chhota Nagpur plateau of India, which, were they transported to a cave of France, would at once be put down as the work of one of the cave-artists, so identical are they in style and treatment. Further, in these Indian paintings there are signs which their discoverer, Rai Sahib Ghosh,** believes are probably traps, though in his monograph he seems unaware of Count Bégouen's researches, and hence the conclusions appear to be independently reached. The Indian rock-paintings also show hunting scenes, the animals drawn with fine sureness of line as in European examples, the men armed with clubs, bows, and arrows. There is not the slightest doubt that their purpose is magical, and I believe (speaking without references on the matter) that South African scholars have reached the same view with regard to the very similar Bushman paintings, which in recent years have excited so much interest.

**Rock-Paintings and other Antiquities of Prehistoric and Later Times (Memoirs of Archaeol. Survey of India, No. 24), Calcutta, 1932.*

There is a drawing in the French cave of Font-deGaume which actually shows a mammoth's weight breaking one of the stakes in a pit; and the pit was the only means the primitive hunter had at his disposal to snare such mighty beasts as the mammoth and the elephant.* Thus the pits are depicted so that by magic the animals would fall into the actual traps.

*Bégouen, op, cit.

We now come to the next step, or a step in some cases contemporary with the paintings: the making of clay models in the round, as at Montespan, where they represent a small bear and several feline creatures, or carvings in relief in the actual rock, as at the Cap Blanc rock-shelter in the Dordogne. The models are literally riddled with stab-wounds, and it is evident, by analogy with Frobenius' modern pygmy hunter's ritual, that the sorcerer would pierce these images with spearheads or flint arrows, pronouncing spells over them to bring death to the beasts of the chase. It is possible that in some cases fresh figures were required to be made for each hunt, but if that were so the scarred image at Montespan is an exception. The heavy onslaught these figures sustained is in line with Mahnowski's insistence on the importance, to the theory of magic, of the simulation by the magician of the real act, and his further insistence on the fact that in the sympathetic emotional condition of the performer lies the fundamental basis of the art; magic is thus, in Malinowski's view, "a ritualized expression of an emotional state of desire".***

***Malinowski, B., on 'Magic, Science, and Religion", in Science, Religion, and Reality (Ed. Needham, 1925).

In addition to the figurines being stabbed in the vital parts, we find numerous paintings and models of animals in the caves lacking ears and eyes, especially the mammoths and the wild cattle; this represents a further development in magical ideas, depriving the animal "by proxy" of those organs which aid it in detecting the presence of its enemy the hunter. This was even carried sometimes to the extent of making the figurine and then sawing off the head, as was done with a statuette of a stag found in the cave of Anléne, Ariége.

It is curious to find that the Egyptian hieroglyphics for certain animals show them decapitated, and some scholars, notably Professor Lam, of Prague University, attributes this to the same magical motive. The Egyptians went a step further, believing that it was possible to transmit to the figure of any living creature the soul of the person or animal that figure represented, and its qualities and attributes. The statue of a god in a temple contained the "spirit" of that god (if we may for convenience use the word "spirit" in this sense), and from time immemorial the Egyptian held that every statue and figure possessed an indwelling spirit. It is at this stage in the story of human beliefs that there occurs the interesting phenomenon of a breaking-down of the borderline, always thin, between magic and religion; for while, putting the matter in very general terms, it may be said that the Egyptian's "religion" was his belief in his corporeal resurrection, his magic was largely directed towards effecting that result by animating the mummy, or the ka statue, to provide for the soul a dwelling-place in his earthly likeness. This is the combination of ideas that has spread throughout the world as the magic of images.

It is but a short step, and a logical one, in this process of reasoning, especially once the principle of using images to give man the power to kill animals for food and for his safety had been established, to the less laudable application of it: the use of the image to bring harm upon a human enemy. It is a branch of sorcery whereof the Egyptians were the originators, and in which they were the greatest adepts of the ancient world. The earliest written account we have of such a use of images is itself as old as the Pyramid Age, is a famous magical book known as the Westcar Papyrus, and concerns the making by a funerary priest of a wax model of a crocodile which was brought to life to wreak vengeance on the paramour of the priest's wife.*

*Erman, Die Marchen des Papyrus Westcar (Berlin, 1890)

The world's most classic instance of the use of wax figures in black magic also comes from Egypt; it is familiar to students as being part of the famous court plot against the life of Ramses III (1198-1167 B.C.);** and the last truly native Pharaoh of Egypt, Nekh-ta-Neb, better known as Nectanebo, was the greatest of all the long line of that country's royal sorcerers, of whose models of ships, used to bring the enemy fleets to grief, the Greek writers tell amazing tales. From Egypt the use of the image in sorcery passed to Greece, and thence probably eastwards with the army of Alexander the Great, who, despite his Napoleonic achievements in ambitious butchery, religiously carted about, everywhere he went, a box of leaden figures, complete with the necessary spells, to bring confusion on his enemies.***

**Breasted, Ancient Records of Egypt (1906-07), vol. iv.

***Bridge, E. A. W., Life and Exploits of Alexander the Great (one-vol. edn.), p. xvi.

We have in the foregoing pages seen some examples of the harmful use of the image in India, notably among the Odiyans of Malabar—that part of the country where one expects, indeed, to find traces of the archaic culture—and it is not uncommon to find this magical procedure figuring in an Indian murder trial. One of the most sensational cases of recent years occurred in the Akola district, in 1934, when the wife of a surgeon, and her alleged lover, a young Rajput assistant in the hospital, were tried for the murder of the medico. The prosecution stated that the couple got an Ojha to make a wax image of the doctor, which he pricked with needles after covering it with vermilion paint to symbolize blood, and buried under the threshold of the doctor's house, in order that the latter should meet with a painful death. The magic proving ineffective, it was alleged that the Rajput finally stabbed the old doctor with a mundane knife.****

    *****Times of India, 24 June, 1934.*

Belief in the death-power of the image is not dead even in the heart of rural England to this day. Some years ago, when working in the Midlands, I went to the wilds of Charnwood Forest, where many strange beliefs survive along with a strong strain of Keltic blood, to investigate a very queer story that the death of a child in one of the lonely villages on the north border of the Forest had been caused by witchcraft. I actually met an ancient hag who was reputedly the village witch, and who showed me a waxen image she had made of her neighbour's child, and who claimed to have caused her death by sticking pins into the effigy and "ill-wishing" her with the aid of incantations, human hair, and nail-parings, and the blood of a cockerel slain at the full moon. Of course, there was no section of the law whereby the police could charge this modern exponent of the most ancient magic in the world, and she knew it! Another of her experiments in black magic was not so successful. Having a grudge against the daughter of another neighbour for a fancied insult, the hag stole a pair of the wench's drawers from the clothesline and boiled them, again with incantations and the blood of a slaughtered cockerel, to render her barren; but the victim married and proved fecund—and the old witch is dead.

Chapter 7

Mysteries of the Serpent

IT has been estimated that at least 30,000 people die annually in India from snakebite; and the Hindu holds the cobra peculiarly sacred—in fact, it is the only snake that, throughout the land, may not be killed with impunity. The figure of Naga Raj, king of all the king cobras in existence, looms large in Hindu mythology, and he is a figure whose existence brings up one of the mysteries of Indian history: the origin of the Naga race, a people who are said to have come from the northwest, to have been half men, half serpents, and to have worshipped serpent-gods. The fascinating question of who they were, and whence they came, we had better leave until later in this chapter, for one can get a far clearer idea of Indian ophic lore and its meaning by considering it in conjunction with beliefs and practices regarding snakes elsewhere.

The rulers of Kashmir and the Raias of Chota Nagpur claim descent from these Naga-folk, who figure prominently in the great epic of the Mahabharata; in the mountainous country bordering on Kashmir, and especially between the Chenab and Ravi rivers, there survives a remnant of the ancient Naga race which has escaped both Islam and the late accretions of orthodox Brahminism. These people do not call themselves Nagas, which was not a tribal name, but an epithet applied to those whose symbol of reverence was the *nag*, or hooded cobra; their tribal name is Takha.* In south India, however, there is a tribe called Nagas, usually described as "primitive", but more probably degraded from a higher civilization, who claim to be descendants of the Nagas.

*Oldham, C. F., "The Nagas", in Journ. Roy. Asiatic Soc., July 1901, pp. 461-473

All over India we fin d the snake temples, but it is important to notice that in every case the worship is not that of a particular cobra as a god, but of certain named serpent-deities, such as Shesha-Nag, Basak Nag, etc., who are regarded as the defied rulers of an ancient people whose symbol—perhaps tribal and totemistic, perhaps racial—was the Naga, or hooded cobra, and whose chief deity was the sun. We shall come back to this point later; it is given here to make clear the meaning of the following Indian legends and beliefs.

The cobra's hood throughout India is regarded as the symbol of royalty, and a child found with a cobra guarding it with outspread hood, or a child bearing a birthmark resembling the hood, was in ancient India immediately assigned royal status, however humble its parents. This has happened within historic times, and several present ruling houses of Indian States owe their position to an ancestor who was a child so singled out, even the rigid principles of caste being waived to allow the precedence—a significant fact, for it shows that the Naga cult, as we may conveniently call it for the moment, is older than orthodox Hinduism; indeed, the demigods of the Takht people today, and the rites attending their worship, are decidedly unorthodox, and their priests are not Brahmins.

According to some ancient Indian writers, the Nagas were really serpents, who could assume human shape at will; this idea, which is a familiar folklore distortion of history, is evident from legends all over the country, which are so similar in their details, and so parallel to stories of the same type elsewhere in the world, as to leave no doubt of their common origin.

One of these concerns the alleged origin of the Rajas of Chota Nagpur, who are styled Nagbansi Rajputs owing to their association with the Nagas. The legend tells how Pundarika, king of the Nagas, took upon himself human form and repaired to the house of a Brahmin at Benares to study the sacred books, in the guise of a Brahmin. He there fell in love with, and married, his host's daughter, but his incarnation was in two respects imperfect: he could not get rid of his forked tongue or his evil-smelling breath. To conceal his halitosis from his bride he always slept with his back to her, which she must have found very disappointing!

Discovering his peculiarities, she promptly evinced the wretched curiosity common to all women; but the snake-king, like Lohengrin (who has the same folklore origin), could only disclose his identity at the cost of losing his wife. He diverted her attention for the time being by proposing a pilgrimage to the great shrine of Jagannath at Puri—which I take to be the ancient Indian equivalent of pacifying your discontented wife by an offer of a week at Skegness! The couple set off through the hills and forests of what is now Chota Nagpur, but when they reached the site of the present town of Ranchi the wife was seized with the pains of childbirth. This seems inconsistent, as her divine husband had always slept with his back to her, but Indian legends are inconsistent. However, her curiosity revived, and she again began asking inconvenient questions. This time she had her husband cornered, and he was compelled to admit that he was actually Takshah Raj, the king of the snakes.

Having divulged his fatal secret, he did not, like Lohengrin, make a dignified exit to the strains of slow music, but at once passed into the form of a gigantic cobra, the shock of which caused his wife to be delivered of a male child and die on the spot. The unfortunate snake made the best of his trying position; spreading his hood, he sheltered the child from the rays of the midday sun, and was thus discovered. One version says the discovery was made by some woodcutters of the Munda tribe, who decided that a child found in such remarkable circumstances must be destined to a great future, and at once adopted him as their leader; another says a Brahmin found the cobra and infant, and that to him the snake told his history and prophesied that the child should be called Phani-Makuta Raja (the snake crowned), and should reign over the count thence to be called Nag-pur. In either case, thus was founded the line of Nagpur Rajas, whose crest is a human-faced, hooded cobra.*

E. T. Dalton, Descriptive Ethnology of Bengal, pp. 165-6.

Again, the Rajas of Manipur, in Assam, trace their descent from a divine snake. At his installation they used to have to pass with great solemnity between two massive dragons of stone which stood in front of the coronation house.

Somewhere within the building was a mysterious chamber, in which was a pipe; this, according to popular belief, led down into the depths of a cavern where dwells the snake-god, ancestor of the royal family. The length and prosperity of the Raja's reign was believed to depend on the length of time he could sit on the pipe enduring the fiery breath of his serpentine ancestor in the place below. "Women", says Hodson, "are specially devoted to the worship of the ancestral snake, and great reverence is paid to them in virtue of their sacred office."**

There is in the Madura district an ancient sacred tank, which contains a broken image of the hooded cobra. Local folklore says that long ago a Raja married a beautiful princess from a distant land, which, however, she was reluctant to leave. Her determination to stay at home grew after marriage, as there seemed to be a cloak of mystery around the figure of her lord; she declared that unless he revealed his lineage to her she would not go with him. At last he had to consent, so he brought her to Madura and took her to the water's edge. Once more he tried to persuade her not to be so curious, as there was a *tabu* on curiosity with regard to the origin of his tribe. The princess, however, persisted, so the Raja began to descend slowly into the waters, warning her constantly that if she showed the least alarm at what she was about to see, she would lose him. Slowly he dived, and then came forth again, this time not as a human being but in the shape of a Naga prince, which indeed he was. His wife shrieked, and at that moment the Naga was turned into stone, "and there he lies to this day to prove it", say the people of Madura.

In Hindu cosmology, the symbol of eternity, infinity, and ultimate absorption in the Great Energy which pervades all things and is the Centre of the Universe is Shesha-Nag, the thousand-headed cobra which is supposed to dwell deep down in the Patal region, or bowels of the earth; on this giant reptile sleeps the preserver god, Vishnu, and it is popularly believed that earthquakes are commonly caused by Vishnu turning in his sleep, thus disturbing the position of his serpent-couch, which supports the earth like Atlas. It was to please this Shesha, according to Plutarch, that a tribal offering was made in ancient times by the sacrifice of an old woman, usually one who had been condemned to death for a crime; she was buried alive on the banks of the Indus.

It is rather remarkable to find that the Bataks of Sumatra have a legend which shows distinct Indian origins—incidentally, it illustrates the eastward spread of beliefs in which earthquakes are attributed to a personage called Naga-padoka*; though no snake is mentioned in the story, he must, by his name, be a distorted form of Shesha, and derive from the same source.

*Frazer, J. G.: Adonis, Allis, Osiris, 2nd edn., p. 165, or The Golden Bough, v, 200.

LOST WORLDS AND UNDERGROUND MYSTERIES OF THE FAR EAST

The Batak legend is that when Batara-guru, the creator, was about to fashion the earth, he began by building a raft, which he commanded a certain Naga padoka to support. While he was hard at work his chisel broke, and at the same time Naga-padoka moved under his burden, whereupon Batara-guru yelled: "Hold hard a moment; the handle has come off my chisel." The creator apparently left his assistant holding up the raft; occasionally he gets fired, and shifts it on his shoulders, causing an earthquake, whereupon the Bataks to this day shout, "The handle, the handle!" to fool him into thinking it is the voice of the creator, and thus getting him to stand still and keep the earth steady.

Though not a folk-tale to account for a tribal origin, a peculiar legend of the Reddi, or Kapu, caste of India deserves notice, for in it features that familiar substance of folklore, the divine nectar. According to this,* one division of the Kapus formerly lived in Ayoclhya— which incidentally is the culture-centre of the kings and heroes in the great epic of the Ramayana— where the discovery of a plot to rob the king caused the hurried departure of Belthi Reddi, with one of his thirteen wives and seventy-seven of his children. In escaping, they had to cross the river Silariadi, which petrified anyone passing through it, so they had to go to a place called Dondakhonda and worship Ganga, the goddess of the holy Ganges, who then helped them to cross the river in safety.

*Miles, op. cit., 131-2

Over the river, they reached the Mallikarjuna temple, where they stayed to help the Jangams, who ruled over it, with the temple duties. Later the Jangams, having to leave for a time, placed the Kapus in charge of the temple; but when they returned, Belthi Reddi refused to hand it over. The contending parties therefore decided that whoever could go to Naga-lokam, the land of the snakes, and bring back the jasmine-flower of snake-land, known as Naga Malligai, should be considered the rightful owner of the temple.

The Jangams decided to go, they being skilled in the magic art of transformation, and went in quest of the flower in spirit-guise. While they were away the Kapus burnt their bodies, and when the spirits returned they had consequently nowhere to enter and dwell. Thereat the god of the temple became very angry, and turned the Jangams into crows so that they might attack the Kapus. The latter, pursued by these carrion-birds, fled to the country of Oraganti Pratapa Rudra, who forced the crows to cease their torment and allowed the Kaapus to settle there as cultivators.

The carpet-weaving caste of Kurubas have a folk-legend in which the cobra appears as a sinister but ineffectual element. They say that the former poverty of their caste so excited the pity of Siva that he left at one house sacred ashes, promising the birth of another son, to be named Undala Padmanna, after whose birth the family at once prospered. Undala, however, was very lazy, and his brothers tried to get rid of him by asking him to set fire to some brushwood near a large ant-hill where they knew a great sacred cobra lived, in the hope that the smoke would cause it to come out and destroy him; but instead of the cobra a large flock of sheep appeared, the sight of which so frightened Undala that he fled. Siva appeared in his path, told him that the sheep had been created for his livelihood, and showed him how to milk them and make curds, and how to shear the animals and weave their wool. The rest of the tale is immaterial to us—it is one of those interminable, dull Hindu stories to account for the superiority of one caste division over another.

Throughout India it is believed that somewhere in the jungle you can never find anyone to specify in which part of the country there exists the real Naga Raj, who is king over all the so-called king cobras, and that he who has the courage to approach this king will be rewarded by the sight of the largest and purest diamond in the world, which Naga Raj carries in his mouth. Thus he figures as the holder of an object familiar in folk-myth, the divine talisman. We shall shortly see the origin and meaning of this belief which is allied to another widespread one that when a big so-called "spectacled cobra", of the variety with "horn-rim" markings round the eyes, is seen, it is guarding hidden treasure.

India, as did the ancient Mediterranean world of whose beliefs its own are a distorted survival, places great credence in the "wisdom of the serpent". Some of the most uncanny stories are told of the long memory possessed by snakes, which, like elephants, are reputed never to forget an injury. I had a personal experience of this when staying in Goa in 1934, when another member of my host's house-party, as we were returning from a walk one evening, foolishly swiped with his stick at a cobra lying on a low stone wall bordering the compound, telling it to go off. Our Portuguese-Indian host was horrified; he said the snake always basked there, had never harmed anyone, and was regarded by the family as quite an old friend; and he declared that it would remember the voice of the man who had insulted it, and would seek revenge. The next evening, when we were sitting in the garden taking a sundowner, this cobra, again in its favourite spot on the wall, heard the man who had slashed at it speaking. It slid down, made a beeline for him, ignoring the rest of us entirely, and bit him in the leg before he could get out of his deck-chair. Luckily for him, medical attention was available.

About the same time as this incident I read in the papers of a curious case from the village of Madampe, Ceylon, where two boys on their way to school rescued from the jaws of a large cobra a hare which it was about to swallow, one boy holding down the snake with a deft stick, as they were unwilling to hurt, it, while the other liberated the victim. As they returned from school later in the day the boys were attacked by the cobra, which had apparently lain in wait at the spot, and one lad died from its bite. The natives declared it had taken revenge for being robbed of its prey.

In Telingana, north India, one must not even call the cobra by its proper name, but must use a euphemistic word, purugu, which means worm, otherwise the snake will haunt one for seven years, and bite at the first opportunity; Bengal holds a similar belief; and natives of Travancore take great care never to speak disrespectfully of the snake, a cobra being called nalla tambiran (The good lord). (See Crooke, Popular Religion and Folklore of N. India, ii, 142; and S. Mateer, Native Life in Travancore, 320.)

Another equally queer report in the papers came from Bina, a town 100 miles from Jhansi, where a G.I.P. railway constable playfully threw a stone at a cobra which crossed his path near his home. The stone hit the reptile, but did not hurt it; but the cobra visited the man's house every day thereafter, seeking to attack him. One day it got its chance, for the constable's wife came in to find him asleep with the brute coiled on his chest, its head reared in readiness to strike when he awoke. She stole out and fetched in several men, including a *sadhu*. When her husband awoke they motioned him to lie quite still, while the holy-man chanted mantras, as the result of which he got the snake to move out of the danger zone.

The constable became unconscious under the strain of this ordeal, and finally lay in a trance, in which he told the *sadhu* the story of his encounter with the cobra, adding that he had been threatened in a vision that if he did not build a stone dais round a certain sacred *nim*-tree the cobra would visit him again and again until it got its revenge. For some days after this the constable delayed building the dais, and each day, until he did so, he saw the cobra round his house; when he built it the creature vanished, and was never seen again.*

Times of India, 26 Jan., 1935

We need only quote one more instance, this time with an element of comedy, the moral of the affair being that you cannot take liberties with a snake's dignity, and that cobras strongly object to being used as dance-partners! In June 1934, Indian officials in Dadu district, Sind, found that a cobra persisted in inhabiting their club-house at Khairpur Nathan Shah. All attempts to turn it out proving futile, they finally sent for a local Brahmin who had a great reputation as a snake-charmer. He enticed it from its lair and captured it, and was so elated with his success that he began to make a tour of the district, holding the cobra in his hands to show off his power over reptiles. When he had, as he thought, got it tame, he took it to a village a few miles away, where there was a temple of Siva, and there, coiling the cobra round his neck, began a Siva dance before the deity's shrine. The loud blowing of the sacred conch-horn, combined with the liberties taken with the cobra's anatomy in the course of the dance, apparently offended its dignity, for it turned on the Brahmin and bit him; he was taken to Larkana hospital in a precarious condition.*

Times of India, 30 June, 1934.

Much sentimental nonsense has been written about snake charmers by the harmful and ignorant type of "author" who lands at Bombay, dashes about the bazaars up and down the country for a month or two, then departs for home and writes an idiotic book on the "mysterious East", replete with the atmosphere of incense, tomtoms, and turbans. The average professional snake-charmer is neither romantic nor sensationally occult. He is usually a none-too-clean wandering conjuror; and the many I have met were all perfectly honest as to the extent of their powers. Some, who possessed undoubted hypnotic influence in other directions, claimed that their hold over the snakes was due to their being able to mesmerize them; others took the view that the snake is physically sensitive to the sound-vibrations set up by the charmer's pipe-and drum music. One of the most intelligent of these men, an old Muslim conjuror whose "pitch" was at Juhu beach, near Bombay, firmly held the latter view, and supported it by quoting the well-known sensitiveness of a snake's motor-muscles, which is such that your bungalow is safe from reptiles if you have around the verandah rough gravel or coco-matting, over which the reptiles will not travel. One of the chief castes with a reputation for snake-charming, by the way, is that of the Kudumi, the rice-pounders of Travancore and Cochin.

As to immunity from snakebite, not one of the charmers I have met claims to be able to confer it on a person, but all of them declare that they themselves are immune through being constantly bitten. This is also given as the reason for the immunity of the priests at the snake-temples, to which, every December, thousands of pilgrims flock to propitiate the demons controlled by the sacred cobras maintained there. On the other hand, one finds many men in India who, without being professional snake-charmers, have the power to quell snake-poison by some psychic power that defies medical explanation.

Miles* records the case of the station-master of a small south Indian railway station who, if advised in time, can cure snakebite by psychic force. He only requires details to be telegraphed to him as to the part of the body affected, and the time and place of the accident, and—the most important part of the information—the direction from the healer in which the event took place, whether north, south, east, or west. It is claimed that this station-master has cured people as much as 500 miles away, after their condition and these facts concerning it have been telegraphed to him.

Op. cit., p. 241.

Weird stories are told of the cures wrought, apparently by supernormal power, at some of the snake-temples of India. There is a famous one at Belgaum, in the Southern Mahratta country, for the details of a "miracle" at which shrine I have the authority at first hand of a European railway engineer who worked in the district for many years. One of his Pathan permanent-way workmen, who, being a Frontier Muslim, had often scoffed at the claims made by his Hindu colleagues for their snake-temple, was bitten by a krait, the little black snake which is one of the most deadly in all India, while working on the track some miles from the town. He was dead within an hour, before his mates could get medical assistance, and when he was carried into Belgaum three doctors said he was certainly dead; the body had gone stiff and started to swell, and nothing could be done for the victim.

The Hindus, however, insisted on taking the corpse to the temple, which is dedicated to Shesha Nag, and where, they claim, the god can even cure snakebite to the extent of resurrection if the body is taken there in time. The men left the Pathan's corpse in front of the shrine all night with a priest chanting mantras over it-and next morning the Pathan "woke up", astonished to find himself there, and without a sign of a bite on his ankle. He went straight off to work, after thanking the priest; he served for many years afterwards in the district, and never scoffed again. Some readers who may themselves scoff at this are probably inconsistent enough, if their judgment is warped by a pro-Christian bias, to admit the miracles of Lourdes. This case is equally real.

My engineer friend investigated the matter closely, thinking that the man may have been in a coma, and that the temple *pujaris* probably used some secret herbal preparation to cure the bite; but they disclaimed the possession of any such knowledge, and, further, the responsible doctors of the district, including an English medical official, declared that when they saw the body it was, in this climate of rapid dissolution, too far gone to make any human aid effective, and that the man was, medically speaking, as dead as they had ever seen anyone!

There are certain people in India who possess extraordinary herbal knowledge of snakebite cures; these are very low jungle tribes, such as the Paliyans and the Nayadi, of whom the latter make special offerings to the souls of their ancestors for protection against the bite. The women of the Valmikudu tattoo their bodies with designs of snakes and scorpions as a sympathetic-magic method of securing immunity—a belief that sometimes leads to fraud by confidence-trickers. In one Namya village, for instance, only a few years ago, a snake-charmer induced three villagers to pay him for tattooing them for this purpose. At a funeral ceremony the next day the tattooer induced one of his clients to hold a venomous reptile. Seeing it bite the villager, the charmer bolted without waiting to prove his charm efficacious, and the victim died soon afterwards.

Not all are swindlers, however; the witch-doctors of the Odde caste of potters are expert snakebite curers, and Miles* describes how one cured a boy bitten on the hand by a cobra. The arm had already grown numb by the time the medicine-man arrived; he threw a brown powder on the spot where the fangs had fastened. He then produced a small wand, which he stuck first into the boy's mouth, then into his own, and then drew it gently up and down the boy's back. All the time the magician uttered strange guttural sounds; gradually the lad's arm became sensitive again, and he began to move his fingers. This went on for several minutes, while the witch-man continued to move the stick up and down his back. Finally the man poured water over the injured hand, and it ran off clean, the powder having evidently been absorbed into the bite; and the boy ran off as though he had never been bitten. The eyewitness of this strange ceremony tried to question the witch-doctor, but could get no explanation out of him beyond vague mutterings about "sap ascending in the trees as the moon waxed, and descending as it waned". It is impossible to find out from these primitive people where the herbal knowledge ends and the magic begins, for the rite means nothing more to them than the medicine, though to us it is inextricably mixed up with the magic.

Op.cit., P. 147

The connection between cures and magic often leads to curious incidents which would be incredible anywhere outside India. One such occurred when in 1934 Ahmedabad Town Council had before it an offer by a man named Dave Gaurishanker Panre that he should be appointed at a monthly salary of 40 rupees (about £3) as the official municipal curer of snake-bite by spells* A medical member, Dr. Hariprasad, moved successfully that the offer be turned down, and suggested that as the Haffkine Institute (the great research centre for poisons and serums) was offering 10,000 rupees reward to anyone who could successfully cure a snake-bitten monkey, Mr. Panre should submit himself to that test of his powers. There was quite a lively debate in the chamber, as the council had just previously accepted an offer from one of its clerks to cure paralysis by a herbal remedy he claimed to have learnt from a *sadhu*, at no cost but that of the drug. As Dr. Hariprasad had supported that proposal, a fellow-member of the council accused him of inconsistency, demanding to know why he gave his backing in the one case to "unscientific, unknown herb", and yet refused to accept the efficacy of magic in the other. Later in the same year I heard that an application had been received by Madras Town Council from Tuticorin municipality, asking for a grant for curing snakebite and disease by mantras, but I do not know the result.

Times of India, 23 Feb., 1934

Another cutting I possess recounts a Ratnagiri Brahmin's fatal faith in mantras plus douches of cold holy-water, when bitten in 1935 by a very poisonous snake of the west coast, whose local name is Phursa. He remained unconscious throughout the magic, then died peacefully.

By contrast we find a firm belief in the efficacy of snakebite itself to cure other ills, and, as is to be expected, it nearly always ends fatally. Among my records is one of a Vizagapatarn Brahmin who had himself intensively bitten by a cobra in the hope of curing consumption, but died of the venom within two hours. Much, however, is being done in Europe on scientific lines in the use of snake-venom, and a report in the **Lancet** for November 1934 aroused wide medical interest. It revealed that part of the venom of the Indian reptile called the Russell Viper was found effective in stopping haemophilia, the bleeding disease from which the Spanish ex-royal family suffers. About the same time, Dr. Harriz, of the Pasteur Institute, Paris, submitted a report to the British Medical Association on his claims to have cured internal growths with cobra venom; and the study of snake serums for the cure of disease is still going on.

These notes, while carrying us slightly away from our subject, are useful as showing that there is very often a scientific basis for some of the most apparently irrational beliefs, though those holding the superstitions may be completely unconscious of it, and may even, like the consumptive Brahmin, apply it in the wrong way.

It is now time for us to examine India's snake-legends and beliefs in the light of those elsewhere in the world, which cast some light upon their significance.

First with regard to the origin of such folk-tales as those to account for the descent of the Rajas of Manipur and of Nagpur, and the turning of the Naga prince into a snake at Madura. Sir James Frazer has shown* that such stories as this all belong to a marked type, the Beauty and the Beast group (as does the operatic legend of Lohengrin).

*The Golden Bough, iv, 125-132 .

As stories of this type are often told by savages to explain why they refrain from eating certain animals, Frazer holds that they were "probably at first told always to explain the totemic belief in the kinship of certain families with certain species of animals", and that when the husband and wife had different clan totems, the violation of the totemic tabus of either might result in their separation—which occurs in this type of tale. He qualifies his totemistic interpretation by pointing out that totemism, or a set of tabus resembling it, must not always be assumed to have existed wherever such stories are told, "for it is certain that popular tales spread, by diffusion, from tribe to tribe and nation to nation, till they may be handed down by oral tradition among people who neither practise nor understand the customs in which the stories originated". He adds, however, that the Manipur story has an analogy: the rulers of Ujjain have for their crest an ass's head, and the legend of their origin is that their progenitor was miraculously born of one who was an ass by day and a man by night, owing to a divine curse. This, says Frazer, may very well have been based on the existence at Ujjain of a line of rulers who had the ass for their totem.

Now, all the stories of this type appear to be based on the "divine marriage" of human beings to gods in animal form which have the power temporarily to assume human form, and are bound up with (a) the survival in folk-memory of the actual slaying of the divine king in the agricultural ritual of the early Mediterranean world, to which we have already given consideration in an earlier chapter; and (b) the belief in the physical fatherhood of a god. There is, though—out the eleven volumes of Frazer's monumental Golden Bough, a great mass of evidence, for which we have no space here, strikingly demonstrating the connection.

As a simple instance, among the Ewe-speaking peoples of the Slave Coast of Africa, the python-god, Danh-gbi, has a body of human wives, the Kosio, who are the priestesses and temple prostitutes, and a close connection exists between the fertility of the soil and the marriage of these women to the serpent-god, for the time when new brides are sought for him is the season when the millet is beginning to sprout; the marriage is deemed necessary to enable him to fulfil his function of making the crops wow; and he is invoked in excessively wet, dry, or barren seasons.*

Frazer, J. G., op. cit., v. 66, quoting A. B. Ellis, The Ewe-Speaking Peoples.

A reminiscence of similar custom appears to be preserved in the fact that among the Takht, the true Naga race of the Himalayan border, there are shrines to the Nagin, or wives of the ancient, deified Naga chiefs**; and in Behar, during the months of Sawan (August), crowds of women go about calling themselves Nagin, or wives of the cobra, ceremonially begging, half their proceeds going to the Brahmins and half being expended in sweetmeats eaten by the whole village.***

** Oldham, C. F., op. cit.

***Frazer, J. G., op. cit., ii, 149, 150

It is widely believed that the "external soul" of a chief or a witch-doctor passes at death into a snake, and that a chief is reincarnated as a snake, or can temporarily inhabit one in life—which no doubt is the explanation of that queer story of Belthu Reddi and the Jangam temple. Here again we seem to have the life of the king, and thus of the tribe and its crops, bound up with the totem, or symbol of the god; which totem, in the case of the snake, is itself closely bound up with fertility, as is illustrated by world-wide customs of rain-magic in which the snake features. The whole of these ideas originated in the Mediterranean region, Egypt in particular, and for a flu exposition of their antecedents I must refer the reader to Elliot Smith's brilliant *Evolution of the Dragon.*

India furnishes us with a good instance of a form of communion with the divine animal in which all may share before slaying, in the practice, very obviously agricultural, of the Mirasans of the Punjab, loosely called a snake-tribe. Once a year, in September, these people worship the snake for a period of nine days. A snake-model of dough is made, painted black and red, and put on a winnowing basket. This they carry round the village, and, on entering any house, utter a blessing and ask for a little cake and butter so that the house will thrive. When all the houses have been visited, the dough snake is buried and a small grave erected over it, and here during the nine days the women come to worship, offering curds at the grave. Here the dough snake is clearly a substitute for a real one; and where snakes abound, the worship is not offered at a dummy grave, but in the jungle, where live reptiles are to be found.*

Punjab Notes and Queries, ii, p. 91, § 555. (March 1885.)

From Egypt by way of Babylonia, where the powers of lifegiving water and earth's fecundity are symbolized in Ea, the water serpent, a group of migrants belonging to what we now call the Archaic Culture must have passed northeastwards, entering India by the Indus and having the Naga as the symbol—totem, if you will—of their priest-kings. The great city of Mohenjo-Daro, to the heights of which, in refinement and sanitation, nothing in subsequent Indian civilization ever attained, is one of the cultural capitals of this northeastward migrating race.

Now, should this sound very far-fetched and theoretical, I would point out the following very curious facts, which I hope to elaborate in a subsequent book. They are here put into print for the first time:

The caste known as Kolis, who are found not merely as a fisherpeople all along the western seaboard of India, but also as agriculturists inland, claim in their own folk-history to have been the servants of the Naga race.

They have their own priests, headmen, and gods, the latter being represented by curious gable-shaped silver plaques called Taks, of which, in the course of long researches among the Kolis with Mr. Vishnu Karandikar, I succeeded in collecting a large number of accurate replicas beaten out for us in copper direct from the originals.*

The very name is suggestive of connection with the Takht race.

These Taks bear, in addition to the figures of the Koli gods, certain symbols which appear to be writing, and which are only found elsewhere in one place: on the cylinder-seals of Mohenjo-Daro.

Some of the Koli gods are shown seated on ceremonial couches of a peculiar character, the design of whose feet, again, is only found at Mohenjo-Daro.

The Kolis preserve a tradition that they and the Nagas "brought the art of writing to India" under a leader called Prithu Wainya. This individual, who figures under the same name in the Puranas, is called The Shining One, and he appears with "the face of an eagle and a body covered with shining fish-scales"; this would appear to mean that he wore a ceremonial eagle-mask, and armour of laminated plates. His description is identical with, and his name analogous to, that of the Babylonian culture-hero Oannes, while the eagle-mask is familiar to us in the sculptures of Mesopotamian priest-kings, who are shown wearing it while engaged in the magical rite of fertilizing the date-palm.

Most striking of all, the sungal, or sacred flail, kept before the Naga shrines of the Takht people, and used in their ceremonial penances, is the exact counterpart, in its design, of that shown in the hands of the Egyptian Osiris, as maybe seen by an illustration Oldham gives of the two flails together.*

Oldham, C. F., op. cit.

Here again we see the Naga, in this association with Osiris, typifying the divine king as the ultimate giver of life, and we thus have an intelligible explanation both for the India-wide belief in Naga Raj holding the peerless jewel in the jungle, and for the part the Nagas play in those great mythico-historical epics, the Ramayana and the Mahabharata. Incidentally, in connection with this aspect of Naga Raj, we may remark that folklore students are familiar with a curious twist whereby old gods, on being dethroned by the conquering of their worshippers, are driven underground, and often, as is very clearly seen in Irish folklore, become gnomes, fairies, or demons.**

*** See Rhys, Mythology of Great Britain and Ireland.*

Naga Raj, king of all king-cobras, is said, in every case save the legend of holding the peerless diamond in the jungle, to dwell deep underground, or under the sea—an interesting association with the widespread "water-dragon" of fertility. It will be recalled that in the earthquake legend we have given, Vishnu sleeps on his giant Naga deep in the bowels of the earth.

Coming now to the epic stories, in the Ramayana, when the monkey-clan chief Hanuman essays to cross from India to Lanka (Ceylon) to rescue Sita, wife of the hero Rama, after her abduction by the demon-king Ravana, one of his enemies is Surasa, mother of the Nagas. Rushing upon him with open jaws, she says mockingly that he must pass though her mouth before he can go any further. Hanuman made himself grow larger, and Surasa's mouth expanded in proportion; the cunning monkey-king then suddenly contracted himself to the size of a man's thumb and jumped through the gap before Surasa could adjust herself, whereupon she good-naturedly acknowledged her defeat. There seems no doubt that Surasa is the ancient water-serpent Ea, in a somewhat unfamiliar guise. The only other reference to the Nagas in the Ramayana is the statement that the terrible demon-king of Lanka, Ravana, had in his time subjugated them among other races which I interpret, like the whole story of the wanderings of Rama, to be a folk memory of a migration from north India to the south, and over to Ceylon, and of tribal battles.

Surasa would appear by her name to be connected with Surya, the sun-god, and this is interesting, for the following reasons:

First, side by side with the worship of the deified Naga chiefs among the Takht of the Himalayan borderland, is that of the sun, which is their chief deity; and second, both the Nagas and the Children of the Sun, whose organization and antecedents betray a Mediterranean origin, are closely connected in the Mahabharata.

This great, if somewhat wearisome, epic is briefly the story of the titanic conflict between two groups of kinsmen, the Pandavas and the Kauravas.

Kunti, mother of the Pandavas and wife of their leader Pandu, has a son by the sungod. Bhima, brother of the great Pandava hero Arjuna of the Bow*, is flung into the Ganges during an internecine feud of this clan. Through the waters, he reaches in the interior of the earth the realm of the serpent-king, who gives him the divine nectar of invincible strength.

*He is the prototype of the Norse hero-archer Aesgil, among other hero-demi-gods.

Arjuna of the Bow is stated in one passage to be the son of Indra; this god, so confused is the pantheon, figures as the rain-deity and enemy of the sun-god in one passage, and as the sun-god himself in another.

We now find Arjuna entering the Ganges for a bath; he is drawn down by Ulupi, daughter of the king of the Nagas, who seduces him, and in return for his copulative services endows him with the power of invisibility in water.

Shortly after this Arjuna, with his brother-in-law, the shining Krishna, who is obviously a human tribal leader later elevated to the position of a god, have a great combat, on behalf of the fire-god Agni, Indra the rain-god and his hosts, and win. Later, when the Pandavas call on the sun-god and receive his aid in their exile after a victory by the Kauravas, Arjuna addresses Krishna himself as "thou who, having floated on the primordial waters, subsequently became Surya"—(and a string of other deities)— "and the firmament and the earth". After further adventures Arjuna rejoins Krishna and the rest of the Pandavas, descending from heaven in the chariot of Indra, who here symbolizes the sun-god.

Finally, when Arjuna is laid low in a terrific combat by his own son, the Raja of Manipura, who cuts off his head, that son himself procures from Naga Raj, who dwells in the bowels of the earth, a certain jewel which, when applied to the dead, brings them to life. Arjuna's head is restored to his body, and father and son are reconciled. It seems quite obvious that Naga Raj here represents a dim folk-memory of an earlier invading race, the Naga-clan, whose divine king was a form of the Osiris, giver of life.

Not the least remarkable part of the Mahabharata is its Indian version of the flood story, which is put into the mouth of a sage, and which in its early stages strongly resembles the Babylonian and biblical stories, with which it of course shares a common Mediterranean origin. The Indian Noah, who builds an ark, is the Rishi (sage) Manu, to whom there finally appears Brahma, lord of creation, in the form of a great horned fish, which tows his ark through the floods and brings it safely to rest on the Himalayas, in gratitude for his having saved and cared for it when it was very small.

Here again is our old friend Ea the water-fertility deity, though in strange guise; here too is the symbolic horned asp of Egypt; and the prototype alike of the Wise Serpent in the oldest stories of mankind, and of the brazen serpent of Israel in the Wilderness.*

*There seems little doubt that the origin of India's peculiar form of worship of the Nagas as deified ancestors is ultimately traceable to the function in the early Mediterranean culture of the "gods-incarnate", or human kings regarded as gods: on which the reader is advised to study the thesis of **The Golden Bough**. This would explain also the idea of the human wives of the snake-gods.

Chapter 8

Beyond the Veil

CERTAIN kinds of occult phenomena are universal in their distribution, and chief among them is the poltergeist, as familiar to England as to the Orient. The spiritualist looks upon the poltergeist as an earthbound "elemental" spirit of low and malevolent intelligence; those occultists who do not accept the concepts and language of spiritualism regard it as a low-vibration form of energy, possibly thought-forms surviving from the disintegration of an intelligence after what is commonly termed "death". In any case, the visible effects of a poltergeist are the same wherever found, and generally consist of a playful tendency to hurl things about, to the discomfort of all concerned—one of the characteristics of the medieval folk-lore figure known as *Puck*.

I encountered some interesting cases of poltergeist phenomena in India. Thus in May 1934 the house of a Punjabi *zemindar* (landowner) in a village near Lyallpur was for three weeks continuously the object of a mysterious attack; every day, about sunset, there came a rain of stones and other brickbats on the roof; they seemed to hurtle out of the sky, and even a strict watch failed to disclose any visible source of the bombardment. Three members of the family were injured, then the rain of stones ceased as abruptly as it had begun.

Similar, and equally inexplicable, was another Punjab case only a couple of months later, when a party of hikers camping at Haran Minara, where they were studying the famous hunting-lodge of the Emperor Jehangir, were bombarded with stones apparently falling from nowhere. This happened for three days in succession, and police officers, who investigated and combed the surrounding area while the stone-throwing was still in progress, failed to discover its source. The students, on returning to

Sheikhapura and making inquiries, found that the Haran Minara building had long had an evil reputation for haunting. A curious feature of the stone-throwing there was that it was always preceded by a noise like the splashing of water.

In Bombay city we had an even more peculiar case, in October of the same year. Here there occurred a downpour of rice, lasting from 8:30 P. M. to 1:30 A. M. for two nights in succession, from the ceilings of the second-floor rooms in a house at Dana Bander, in the Indian town. I visited the place and investigated fully; the whole of the ceilings were intact, and no rice was stored above them, so the work of a practical joker appears to be ruled out, especially as the families living in these one-room tenements all got treated equally to the rice-shower at the same time, and most of them were asleep, with their doors bolted, when it began. After the second visitation the terrified Hindu tenants sent for an astrologer, who, though unable to explain the mystery, performed certain rites and hung up a lemon and a coconut from the ceiling to break the spell; there was certainly no repetition of the occurrence after that.

When there is no apparent motive, these incidents are attributed in India to the malevolence of a *bhut*, or evil spirit; when there is one, the poltergeist phenomena are ascribed to the human agency of black magic. An Indian friend related to me such a case within his own experience in Malabar, when staying there a few years ago with his uncle. The uncle had a dispute with a neighbour over the boundary of a paddy-field, and the parties took the matter to court. While the case was *sub judice*, but with every prospect of its ending in favour of my friend's uncle, a bombardment of stones one night rained on the house, battering the doors and smashing the windows, when the whole family had retired. Naturally, suspicion fell at once on the litigious neighbour; but, despite an immediate and thorough search in and around the compound, not a soul could be found. The nuisance was repeated every night for a week, and culminated in a daytime bombardment in which stones fell clean though the thatched roof with great force. This was the last manifestation; the disturbance ceased while the case in court was still in progress, and investigation showed that the neighbour could not possibly have been responsible.

It is very usual to find a poltergeist force being concentrated on, and, indeed, centred in, one particular person. When this occurs the Indian peasant of course says that person is possessed of an evil spirit, or is being cursed or haunted; the western student of psychophysics takes the view that such a person is (on the analogy of radio) a kind of "receiving-set" unfortunately attuned to the reception of these wave-vibrations, and thereby a medium which releases them into tangible activity.

A remarkable case came to light in April 1934 at the village of Kanhur, near Ahmednagar, where, it was revealed, a peasant's daughter-in-law had been "haunted" for two years being subject to violent attacks from some unknown force. While working, the woman would suddenly find herself being strangled, and discover round her neck a "lamp-string" of the type used for tying corpses to the bier, while her body was covered with black lines and crosses, apparently made by the *bibba*, a nut used in the same way that we use marking-ink. A well-known Ahmednagar lawyer, who was also a landowner of some standing in the village, assured me that he was actually present in the house when one of these weird attacks was made on the woman. He saw the corpse-string appear round her neck from nowhere, and saw her coil of hair (worn at the nape of the neck by Hindu women) cut off, as by an invisible knife. Finally, *bibba-seeds* fell out of her mouth. Peculiar features of these attacks were that the woman remained always completely conscious throughout her ordeal, and that her visitations only occurred on Tuesdays, Thursdays, new moon, and full moon. They apparently had no relation to her periodicity. On some occasions her husband and children also found the black *bibba*-markings on their bodies at the same time; and friends had to keep a close watch over the woman to see that she was not strangled.

There was a strange end to this haunting: Hindu sympathizers sent the family some sacred ashes, known as *bhasma*, and a Christian priest sent a handkerchief which had been blessed; and thereafter there was no repetition of the trouble. I would not like to hazard a guess as to which of the two "chain's", if either, was the efficacious one!

Another interesting case of connection between a poltergeist and a specific person came from the village of Thakurganj, in north Bengal, during the same year. For about a month stones rained down on the roof of the kitchen at a depot there but only when one particular cook, a man named Golap Jha, was on the premises. The facts of t is were confirmed by Babu Satish Gandra Das Gupta, the chief officer of the depot, and by Dr. Tincowri Sarkar, the medical officer in charge of the local hospital, and finally Press representatives were invited to a demonstration. The cook, then working in a nearby bazaar, was fetched in, after men had been placed all round the outside of the kitchen, in a cordon, to see whence came the stones. As soon as Golap jha took his seat on the verandah, a large stone fell with great force on the corrugated-iron roof of the kitchen. Asked whence it came, the watchers outside declared they only saw it when it was about two feet from the root hurtling down. The stone was fetched down from the roof and examined, and all present agreed that there was none like it to be found in the village, and that it must have come from the bed of the Mechi river, a mile and a half away. A few minutes later there was another great noise, and this time two bricks were seen to fall from the sky on the roof. The terrified cook fled back to his bazaar, saying he feared to remain in a spot where he had evidently "disturbed the spirit". The man had worked for the depot officer for nearly eighteen months before this manifestation began; it only happened when he was in the kitchen, and did not occur in other buildings in association with him.

This was quite to be expected, for the restriction, or concentration, of the supernormal activity is a familiar feature in cases of this kind. I once investigated one in England, in which a small schoolgirl suddenly became the force-centre of a poltergeist energy which flung furniture and crockery about in her home; when she was removed to a relative's house the manifestation in her own home ceased, and it did not accompany her to that of the relative. In this case the "haunting" was accompanied by the materialization of a hairy, apelike arm, which threw off the tablecloth. After long investigation by myself and several other occultists, we traced the trouble to a beam in the child's bedroom, which beam had come from the village mill, where the miller of half a century before had hanged himself. On our advice the father took the beam out and burned it, and thereafter all visitations ceased. Here is a clear instance of a low thought-form, apparently surviving from the personality of the suicidal miller, remaining attached to the beam by some "wave-process" that we do not yet understand, and becoming transformed into a malevolent form of energy through the body of the little girl, who, unfortunately for her, possessed vibrations that made her an appropriate "transformer" or receiver.

From Bengal we may next turn to some incidents at the other end of India—Malabar, which has an intense belief in the evil spirits known as Kuttichchathans, or "satan?", which are said to be a gnomelike spirit-people, very small in build, incurably mischievous, and nearly always on bad terms with human beings. The witch-doctors of Malabar are daily kept busy exorcizing persons, places, and houses from their hoodoo.

A Travancore schoolmaster. Mr. K. Venkateswaran, to whom I am indebted for many details of south-Indian beliefs, told me of a weird experience he had some years ago when staying in a Travancore house with friends for a couple of months. They could hardly ever get a night's undisturbed rest, owing to the weird sounds coming from the upper storey of the house, whence emanated the dull thumping noise of paddy-husking by means of a pestle and mortar.

Although they often paid sudden visits to the attic, there was nothing to be seen to account for the noise, which stopped as soon as the investigators reached the door, and recommenced when they had descended. After a few weeks the manifestations became worse; weird bluish fire was seen on the surface of the house tank, with sounds of weeping and wailing coming from its midst, and the disturbance became so bad that the friends finally left the house.

The same scholar told me of a curious case of possession in a Travancore village, where a woman of respectable family, who was not normally strong, suddenly became possessed of amazing physical strength, being able, for instance, to lift up a heavy household table with one hand. Also, she continually produced from beneath her bed articles she and other members of the household had missed, and had thought stolen, some years before—although, on each occasion, there was nothing under the bed a few minutes before. Her neighbours declared that Kuttichchathan was at the bottom of all this, and fetched in a trusted local magician, who performed a succession of weird rites, after which the woman was freed from her trouble and became normal again.

Mr. Venkateswaran investigated for me a sensational occurrence in a village of Central Travancore in May 1933 and from his report this seems to have followed the normal course of poltergeist activity, a young girl being the "victim". Stones hurtled at the house from nowhere; when rice was boiling in the kitchen, the cooking pot suddenly became fouled by unidentifiable foreign matter with an overpowering stench; and the young girl seemed to become possessed, using obscene language and terrible threats, of which she later had no knowledge.

Several exorcists wrestled with the evil, and one finally claimed to have made the "spirit" promise it would leave the house and the body of the girl; so the next day the men of the house went off to theft work in the fields, thinking there would be no more trouble. Hardly had they gone, however, when the girl was again possessed, abused the other women of the family, and said, in a voice totally unlike her own (and claimed to be that of the evil spirit): "You are trying to drive me away; you shall see what comes of it." At that moment the house burst into flames, and it was nearly destroyed before help could be procured; the girl made several attempts to throw herself into the flames, and had to be locked in an outhouse for her own safety. When the fire was subdued, however, she was missing; she was later found sitting, unburned, in a half-gutted room of the house.

Frequently a hoodoo attaches to a building rather than to a person. Whatever be the explanation, it is a fact that some houses do hold an evil influence, as I can personally testify, having lived in one here in staid England until it became utterly intolerable. There is a flat in a house in Ripon Road, Bombay, where every tenant has either met with misfortune or left in disgrace. A railway engineer who lived in it lost his job and several members of his family soon after moving in; the next tenants, a young married couple, drifted swiftly into discord, and the wife left with all her husband's belongings; then came a restaurant-keeper, who, soon after moving in, lost his business and was ruined, and had to "flit" one night without paying his rent; and, finally, a personal acquaintance of mine, poohpoohing superstition, took the flat. When he went there he was in fairly comfortable circumstances; he soon fell into bad health and financial trouble. He developed a violent temper, resulting in daily discord between himself and his wife; and the affair might have ended in tragedy had he not had a friendly chat with the rent-collector, who advised him to move elsewhere. He did, and his affairs immediately returned to normal prosperity and happiness.

Indians have a curious belief that three-cornered houses are particularly unlucky. Buildings of this queer structure are common in towns like Bombay, where space is cramped, and houses are put up on every available corner of land. I know of several "triangular" houses in that city which bear an evil reputation for their tenants meeting with misfortune. Of course, we have in England a famous thee-cornered house, the Triangular Lodge at Rushden, Northants, built by Sir Thomas Tresham in honour of the Trinity, with all its doors and windows in threes. It certainly did not bring him good fortune, as he lost his head in Gunpowder Plot.

LOST WORLDS AND UNDERGROUND MYSTERIES OF THE FAR EAST

Returning to supernormal influences on people I have in my records a peculiar affair from Kolhapur, in July 1934. Here a woman named Anandibai, wife of R. B. Majumdar, was discovered missing from her bed one night when the household was aroused by the crying of her three-months-old baby, which slept with her. Search revealed her floating out in the middle of the sacred Mankarnika Tank, near the Mahalaxmi temple, calling out the word "Narayan".

Her face, breast, and the front part of her sari were quite dry. It took her some time to come to her senses; she was then got to the shore, as she could not swim, holding on to a bamboo pole. When she recovered, she said all she knew was that someone lifted her from her bed, carried her through the air, and laid her on the water, the cold touch of which woke her. The village, of course, declared she had been carried off by a spirit.

To supernatural circumstance was ascribed the death of an outcaste youth in a Punjab village in November 1934. Apparently in the best of health, he had occasion to visit a graveyard, where he picked up a piece of white cloth from the ground to clean his hands. They at once swelled up; the youth dashed home, lay down, went into a trance, and declared that he belonged to the company of the spirits and that none should interfere with him. A sorcerer tried to expel the devil, but the youth died within two hours. On reading this tale in the papers, I thought the victim must have contracted some disease from the rag, as one might easily do in an Indian graveyard, but, if so, the action must have been remarkably swift; unfortunately, it was impossible to get any more exact details of this interesting case.

Among miscellaneous phenomena which admit of no scientific explanation must be placed what Sherlock Holmes might have called "the case of the fiery tree". This concerns a flint-tree which stands in the middle of the grain market at Rupar, in the Ambala district of the Punjab. About 11 o'clock on the night of Sunday, 10 June, 1934, there began a heavy shower of fiery sparks falling from the top of the tree. After continuing for about half an hour, it suddenly ceased, and close examination showed not a trace of fire, ashes, charcoal, or even singeing either of the tree or the ground; nor could any trace of gunpowder or potash be discovered. One old resident then recalled that the same phenomenon occurred at the same tree forty-three years before.

The *nim* is sacred throughout India, and always held to be the abode

131

of a spirit very often, in the jungle, of tribal ancestors. An aged *nim-tree* in Myingyan, Burma, at the end of 1934, suddenly surprised the residents by taking on the functions of a toddy-palm, for it began exuding a potent sap indistinguishable from toddy, to the extent of a gallon and a half daily. Invalids of the district claimed relief after drinking this "nectar of the gods", the provision of which they attributed to beneficent *nats* (the Burmese term for spirits) inhabiting the old tree. Possibly botanical examination would have disclosed a perfectly natural reason for the nim's apparent change of function, but no scientific explanation can be given for a class of malevolent hauntings we shall now consider.

Kandy, Ceylon, has a notorious railway bridge, from which countless people have fallen by accident or suicidal intent; when an inquest was held on a victim in July 1934 the police stated that they had found tufts of black hair jammed under the railway sleepers to act as a charm against the evil. Two months later a Bombay merchant's agent fell off this bridge, making the tenth victim in that year alone; and all Ceylon firmly believes the bridge is haunted.

I have had unpleasant personal experience, as also have several acquaintances, of a singular hoodoo spot in Bombay. This is a point on the seaboard drive known as Hornby Vellard, immediately opposite a place known as Haji Ali's Durga, an ancient Muslim shrine built in honour of Haji Ali, a *pir*, or saint, who was drowned there; the shrine stands on a little promontory out in the sea. On several occasions, driving past this spot in the small hours of the morning, I have felt myself enveloped in what seemed like a patch of ice-cold air, though the night temperature was never much below eighty degrees, and have felt my wrists gripped by cold, steel-like hands, and the steering-wheel forced sharply over towards the footpath and palm-trees. On two of these occasions I found blue bruise-marks on my wrists, which were even there next morning; and another time on approaching this spot I found another European who had come to grief at it, with his car-bonnet nuzzling a palm. He had experienced exactly the same feeling as myself and he also had bruises and claw-like marks on his wrists. It seems very peculiar that this malevolent influence, whatever it is, should exist near the shine of a saint.

This, however, was nothing compared with the ordeal that befell a girl dancer friend of mine; it forms perhaps the weirdest of all the ghost-records I collected in India, and it provides a very curious instance of what is known as "mass-haunting". After performing in cabaret at Ahmedabad one night in January 1935, the dancer drove out alone for a breath of air along the road between Chindola Lake and Kankaria Lake. Here, when she reached a spot where one side of the road is lined with ancient Muslim tombs, and on the other stand the ruined wall and *aiwan* (gate) of an ancient mosque, she was astonished to see a figure in white standing right in the path of the car. Hooting failed to make it move, so my friend pulled up. Only then did she realize it was not some straying peasant in his white *dhoti*, but a transparent figure nearly twice life-size.

This apparition suddenly vanished; the *danseuse* then saw a glow of flame on her right, and on looking closely, was amazed to see a fierce duel in progress round a fire up against the mosque wall, the combatants being attired in costumes she had never seen worn during a lifetime spent all over India. Later, when describing the experience to an Indian scholar, she was informed that they were costumes of Mughal times (the late seventeenth century).

One of the duellists swished at the other's head with a great scimitar, decapitating him; to her horror, the danseuse saw the headless body, spouting blood from the neck, dash straight at her car. Though normally, I know, she has nerves of steel, she screamed and fainted. When she came round, she found herself still seated in the car, with the switch-key in her hand, ditched in a field some twenty feet off the road; and to this day she does not remember driving it there, while, to add to the mystery, the car had gone clean across a fairly deep *nullah*, or roadside ditch.

My friend managed with difficulty to get the car back on the road, by which time the fire and figures had vanished. Determined to investigate the affair, she drove out again in the morning, but could find no trace of a fire, ashes, or blood against the mosque turns. Historical records threw no light on the matter, but local tradition said that at some vague time during the Mughal occupation there was a fight outside the mosque in which a man was beheaded, and that the road at this spot was said to be haunted.

However, there was a sequel, which showed that the danseuse had evidently had a very narrow escape from some elemental force. She mentioned her experience to a German friend then in Ahmedabad, who had studied occult phenomena very deeply, and he agreed to drive her out to the place again next night. As they approached, she begged him to turn back, feeling that something terrible and evil lurked there, but he reassured her and drove on.

Arrived opposite the mosque wall, they both heard a horrible, uncanny laugh, and the girl lost consciousness. Her German companion told her later, when they were safely back in Ahmedabad and she had recovered from the shock, that just as they heard the laugh he saw a pair of black hands descending over the back of the open car to clutch her throat.

His knowledge saved her, for, knowing the fact, familiar to occultist; that steel dispels elemental emanations, he had taken with him a dagger. With this he attacked the ghostly hands as they gripped the girl's throat, and they instantly vanished. The danseuse, however, had blue marks and deep claw-like dents round her throat for some days afterwards.

There seems no doubt that here survived evil thought-forms from a deed of violence, capable of transmission into dangerous activity with this particular person as an unconsciously attuned medium. Very different in spirit and character was a survival of thought-form experienced in Malabar by my Brahmin friend Vishnu Karandikar, some of whose researches I have already recounted in the foregoing pages. Some years ago, unable to complete his journey to schedule owing to bad weather, and having to travel upriver, he found himself more or less marooned one evening, arriving at sunset at a village. From the boat he espied a well-built house that looked unoccupied, and asked his boatmen, local men, if they thought there would be any objection to his spending the night there. They looked queerly at each other and merely shrugged their shoulders, so he proceeded to unload his camp-bed and impedimenta, and went up to the house, the front door of which stood open.

As soon as Mr. Karandikar got inside, a courteous old *pandit*, who seemed to be about seventy years of age, rose from an Indian swing and welcomed him, speaking, rather to my friend's surprise, in Sanskrit instead of the Hindi *linguafranca* usual today even among Brahmins. Soon the conversation took a very peculiar turn. Learning that Mr. Karandikar had come from Maharashtra (the Mahratta country), the pandit said casually, "By the way, I suppose Baji Rao 11 is still Peshwa in Poona?" Then my friend realized what he had begun to suspect, that he was talking to a spirit or a thought-form-for Baji Rao II, last ruler of the mighty Mahratta Empire, abdicated in 1818.

Quickly recovering from the shock of this realization, Mr. Karandikar decided he had an unrivalled opportunity here, and he carefully avoided the risk of dispelling the thought-form, by replying that he himself had been away from Maharashtra for some time, deep in his studies, and really did not know the latest political developments there. The pandit went on chatting familiarly of events we know to have happened between 1790 and 1816, as though he had been at Poona the day before, and finally remarked, "I too seem to have lost touch; you see, I had an accident. I fell into the river down there, and do not remember anything about it, except that I found myself back in my own house."

He then bade his guest good-night, after leaving food with him. The next morning he was not to be found to be thanked for his hospitality; and when Mr. Karandikar investigated the local records, he discovered that a pandit who owned the house was actually drowned in the river in front of it over a hundred years ago. Since then the house was reputed to be haunted, and the village took the view that if you slept there you did so at your own risk. Feeling that some part of the old scholar's personality might be earthbound to the spot because his tragic death had rendered it impossible to give him his Brahmin funeral with Vedic rites, as the body was never found, Mr. Karandikar performed the necessary rites at the house before leaving.

Experiences such as this, and that which befell Mr. Karandikar and myself with the image of Gayatri at Mahableshwar, as related in an earlier chapter, cannot be explained by western science. It were foolish, indeed, to deny, when one has the evidence of one's own eyes, that there does exist a great deal of occult influence, both good and evil, in the ancient holy places of India. To understand how and why both should occur together, it is necessary to know something of basic Hindu philosophy. So much utter nonsense has been written by Europeans on the subject that I feel justified in giving here certain statements of the Hindu esoteric view. I believe this is the first time such a direct, first-hand statement has ever appeared in print, and I am enabled to give it by the courtesy of a very learned Brahmin priest on the one condition that his anonymity is respected, solely because he has a horror of all publicity and controversy, which is why the European, even though he be a seeker after truth, can rarely get a priest to make any serious utterance on the matter for publication. My friend says:

"In our ancient holy places, we Brahmin students of occult wisdom find, still existing, powerful surges of forces, which are of different types and age;

they exist almost, as it were, in strata, each with its distinctive 'colour-tone'. This is a fact of which you western occultists are partly aware when you speak of the colour of an aura surrounding a person.

"These forces each respond to their complementary vibrations in thought and sound; this is understandable if you think for a moment of the Tibetan use of the 'symbol of perfection', Om, and the cumulative vibration its mass-repetition produces.

"At the temple on Parvati Hill, at Poona, which was made the chief centre of Hindu revivalism by Nanasaheb Peshwa in 1739-49, seven underground cellars have been discovered by excavation. There arose in these, by the use of the appropriate mantras, seven distinct types of psychic notes, which were intended to build up a harmonious totality for those who believe in these ancient 'words of power'—the existence and force of which (magical, if you care to call it so) were recognized in ancient Egypt.

"Meditating in this place, I sensed layers of powerful forces; those in the earliest strata seemed 'colourless', but the later ones, deepening in colour-tone, were mixed with dull, red-brown, sediment-like emanations, indicating earthbound, physical sex radiations of the type controlled in the exercise of the lowest form of yoga, the prayana-yoga. These, however useful they may have been in the primitive stages of mankind's culture, in connection, for instance, with the ensuring of the earth's fertility, were certainly out of place even in the eighteenth century.

"It was this gradual deterioration in the use and application of the mantras which developed and intensified in these seven cellars on Parvati Hill. Why? Because man does not always realize the possibility of an individual, who is being used as a means of working these words of power, being coloured by personal desires of a purely physical type. His personality not only destroys the efficacy of the vibrational Power-Harmony which is being created, but also causes its loosening into disruptive and often malevolent activity. Thus apparently was nullified the definite plan on which, as the construction of the Parvati temple and the whole of those hilltop buildings indicates, a powerful yantra was being formed and vitalized by the chanting of mantras.

"Just as, in the early years of the Christian era, King Samudragupta performed the Horse Sacrifice as indicating the revival of the ancient sacrificial type of Hinduism, or as Harsha in the sixth century performed austerities and gave away all in charity to revive the charity aspect of Hinduism, so in the eighteenth century did Nanasaheb Peshwa attempt the revival of the esoteric forms on Parvati, to provide militant Hinduism with a potent weapon against militant Islam. That was why he even moved his capital from Satara to Poona, and Parvati became the centre of spiritual power.

"This cumulative power grew; but with it grew the danger, caused by the intrusive emanations of what I should call the unpure, the individuals operating the mantras, who were not free of the earthbound attachment; thus the power disintegrated into a disruptive force for evil, and the worship degenerated into the *sakti*, which is based purely on the gratification of the sex impulse, and which results in the orgies that so disfigure much of our practical Hinduism of today. By a poetic justice, the result was the breaking of the Maratha power forever at the battle of Panipet. It is, frankly, the task of us Brahmin priests to abolish the stigma, and, by cleansing our worship from *sakti*, to weaken the resistance of these emanations that are wholly evil. "

How true this is, the average Englishman, drugged into an unthinking stupor by his mass-tastes—his standardized radio, cinema, football—will probably have difficulty in realizing, if indeed he has the brains to bother to think on the matter at all. The few who do not let their minds lie in the rut, however, will be convinced by the evidence of first-hand experience, such as fell to my own lot in company with this same Hindu priest whose notes I have just quoted, as to the incalculable, evilly potent mind-forces that survive in the world from other ages.

In the course of my archeological work in India I had the good fortune to discover the site of the ancient city of Pun, which in the twelfth century of our era was the capital from which the Northern Silaharas ruled over their small empire of the Deccan. There was but one slight literary clue in ancient Indian records as to its probable site, and this led me to search in the desolate scrub country some fifteen miles east of Bombay. To my wife wholly belongs the honour of "drawing first blood" in the discovery, as she noticed an ancient carved stone when, in hunting for the site, we got the car stuck in the sandy wilderness near the village of Marol. This led to explorations resulting in our discovery of building-ruins extending over an area of some two square miles, and finally, in the midst of it, a large temple site.

When it came to getting labour, however, we could not induce a single

Indian to go near the place, even the Indian Christians (whose alleged Christianity is of a very superficial and barbaric order). All declared the spot was accursed and that, varyingly, the gods or demons dwelt there, and would wreak vengeance on anyone touching any of the stones-despite the fact that the site contained a couple of ancient sacred Hindu tanks, and several images of the elephant-god Ganesh among the undergrowth. At this time, apart from such stray fragments of sculpture, there was nothing to be seen aboveground but a great verandah-like platform with a balustrade of stone lattice-work some hundred feet long, and, some distance from this, the outline of foundations of a small building only some twenty-four feet square.

So we set to work to do our own excavating, a gruelling task in a temperature of well over a hundred, and after a fortnight's work we unearthed the ground-plan of a typical shrine dedicated to the sexual *sivalinga* worship. That is, its layout was typical in all but one respect—the pointed-oval base for the lingam faced the wrong way; the shrine entrance was at the wrong end; and so were the footing blocks of the *mandrapaisa*, or pillared hall in front of the shine. In short, it reminded one strongly of the ritual arrangements for the Black Mass in medieval Europe, in which the ecclesiastical Mass was travestied, said backwards, with black candles and obscenities decorating the altar.

My wife thereafter flatly refused to visit the spot, saying she felt an influence around it that was wholly evil; and I too felt this unseen force. In clearing the debris outside the shine itself we had, a few days before, found a tall oblong pillar inscribed with a land-grant of a date corresponding to A.D. 1172, and bearing a carving, familiar in Indian archeology, known as the "ass-curse", intended to lay a curse on anyone interfering with the terms of the grant. This sculpture depicted one of the worst imaginable sexual abortions of a disgusting nature hardly to be described in a book such as this. Two peasants whom we finally persuaded to take a truck up for the purpose of removing this land-grant to the Prince of Wales Museum fled in terror the minute they set eyes on the *sivalinga* shrine newly excavated close by, declaring that it was inhabited by an evil spirit, and nothing would induce them to do the job; in the end, in fact, I had to turn over the whole site to the museum on leaving India, and leave its staff to wrestle with the problem of getting the stone shifted.

After these discoveries I got in touch with my priest friend, knowing him to be deeply learned in black magic and Sanskrit, for the purpose of finding out more about this evil shrine. We went there on the night of the full-moon festival, and on the *sivalinga* base the priest performed certain Tantric rites, involving the use of incantations and a bowl of pig's blood, a well-known substance in occult ritual for causing the materialization of elemental forms.

As I have hinted in speaking of the poltergeist, it is not necessary to regard these "elementals" as the actual disembodied spirits of persons evil in life, or even as discarnate intelligences, so much as thought-forms, so powerful that they have persisted through the ages. This is the view of "ghosts" as set forth forty years ago by Hudson, in his brilliant **Law of Psychic Phenomena**, written before wireless had become an established fact, but, in its theory, bearing striking analogy to what we now know of radio wave-action. Baird, our television pioneer, declared not long ago that if we had the radio apparatus powerful enough we could recapture the words even of Henry VIII, which are still somewhere in the universe as soundwaves. Such an analogy may well be used in considering thought-waves, for they too are indestructible, and, when impinging on a living personality attuned to the right wavelength, as it were, are in some cases susceptible of materialization into the form of the personalities that sent them forth—in vulgar parlance, ghosts. That is why it is possible calmly to believe that powerful maledictions uttered with the effective vibration coefficients in ancient Egypt, and concentrated into effective malevolence by a magic, or a science of psycho-physics, the West has lost, may yet wreak havoc on modern disturbers of Egyptian tombs.

To return to our shrine. Gradually out of the smoke of the incense, hovering above the libation of blood poured out into the central hollow of the lingam base, there appeared vague, pillarlike shapes floating mistily across the moon, but remaining outside the circle of protection the priest had made, and within which we stood. Two of these wraiths eventually took a form nebulously human, though no features were distinctly visible, and voices spoke in a sibilant whisper. As the conversation was conducted in Sanskrit, which I do not understand, my priest friend, who made notes while it was in progress, translated it to me afterwards as follows (sometimes one thoughtform spoke, sometimes the other):

WRAITH: *We are summoned by the offering of Lord Siva. What do you want with us? Why do you call us here?*

PRIEST: We would know the meaning of this shrine.

WRAITH: *Can we not go hence? Are we ever bound here?* [This was apparently a protest at being earthbound to the spot.] *It is a shrine of Lord Siva, whose power ye surely know.*

PRIEST: This we know. We would know why it is all placed backwards. All the shrines of Lord Siva are not thus.

WRAITH: *It is the shrine of the most hidden heart of Siva, that worketh in darkness for man. Darkness that is death whereof cometh life. It is not good that ye know of it more, for the knowledge bringeth death. Yama* [the god of death] *sleeps not.*

PRIEST: Why worked ye the things of death in this place?

WRAITH: *We were the priests of Lord Siva, and as he bid us, so did we. All in life standeth in the balance with death. Of both sought we the secrets.*

PRIEST: Why does the evil of this worship still cling to this place?

WRAITH: *What call ye evil? Evil and good are one. Death is not evil; it is the gate of maya* (oblivion]. *Our lives were bound up with this shrine. Our thoughts cannot die. They it is that are still here. It is our thoughts to which you speak.*

PRIEST: All men fear this place and avoid it. What did ye here?

WRAITH: *I have told thee; we did the puja* [worship] *of Lord Siva, he that demands blood of the world to renew the world.*

PRIEST: Then these stones are stained with the blood of men?

WRAITH: *What would ye? All life is sacrifice. Must not the god feed even as men? By blood ye have summoned us.*

PRIEST: When was this shine made?

WRAITH: *When here was a great city that the Silaharas made.*

PRIEST: What date was that?

WRAITH: *We know not what ye mean by date and time. Thought is timeless. The god is timeless. Always we dwell here, we thoughts; we cling.*

PRIEST: Where dwell ye now?

WRAITH: *We know not what ye mean by that. The bodies that we dwelt in lie yonder in samadh* [trance]. *They were priests here. We are the thoughts of them that ye have made to speak by your Tant* [magic]. *Always dwell we here, with Lord Siva.*

Further questions only produced the same kind of answers, and it was evident that we had exhausted the capacity or will of these ancient thought-forms for further communication.

That they were utterly evil there can be no doubt; one could feel them trying to get at us, engulf us, could feel them growing angry at their impotence to break the circle of protection. The priest wisely felt it was time to desist, before their vibrations became too strong, and perhaps uncontrollable, and he dematerialized them with mantras and his ancient ritual. I had a feeling of intense, cold terror during the whole of the ceremony, and was frankly glad when it was over and we could safely leave the shrine and return to the civilization, poor as it was, of Marol village.

That was the last time, knowing what I do of oriental occultism, that I ever went near the shrine—a pity, perhaps, from the purely archeological point of view; but there are some sites that are better not disturbed, and if ever there was one in which a persistent tradition of living mana was justified, it is this site. As for the ritual my priest friend employed to materialize the thought-forms of eight centuries ago, I have the full details of it—but they are locked up, and there they will safely remain. There are some things in this great, mysterious India upon which it is best, for the safety of the human soul, to let the curtain fall.

The End

143

144

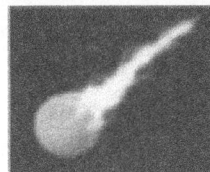

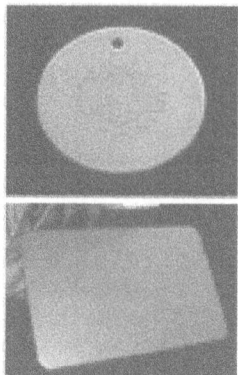

146

152

153